Long Beach Island, N. J.

Picturing
Long Beach Island,
New Jersey

The Return of the Fishing Boats in Surf, Long Beach Island, N. J.

The Dock   Beach Haven, N. J.

Beach Haven, N. J.
The Engleside from The Tennis Courts

Schiffer
Publishing Ltd

Glenn D. Koch

4880 Lower Valley Road   Atglen, Pennsylvania 19310

Photograph, Dogs & Dunes, with Water Tower, Beach Haven, N.J. c. 1960. $20-30

This book is dedicated to the memory of John Bailey Lloyd, 1932-2003.
Wherever he is, I am sure that every hour there is Happy Hour!
And it is also dedicated to the memory of Betty Gangwere Tombaugh, 1932-1992.
She spent fifty one weeks of her year waiting for her one week on Long Beach Island.

Other Schiffer Books on Related Subjects
Cape May Gingerbread Gems. Tina Skinner & Bruce Waters
Cape May Point. Joe Jordan
Cape May Point: Three Walking Tours of Historic Cottages
Cape May Postcards
Collector's Guide to Trenton Potteries. Thomas L. Rago
Doorways of Cape May. Tina Skinner & Melissa Cardona
Gingerbread Gems. Tina Skinner & Bruce Waters
Gingerbread Gems of Ocean Grove, NJ. Tina Skinner
The Ocean City Boardwalk: Two-and-a-Half Miles of Summer.
  Dean Davis
The Sand Lady: A Cape May Tale. Corinne M. Litzenberg &
  Bari A. Edwards, Illustrator
Touring New Jersey's Lighthouses. Mary Beth Temple & Patricia
  Wylupek

Copyright © 2007 by Glenn D. Koch
Library of Congress Control Number: 2007924093

Designed by Mark David Bowyer
Type set in Americana XBd BT / Aldine 721 BT

ISBN: 978-0-7643-2705-6
Printed in China

Published by Schiffer Publishing Ltd.
4880 Lower Valley Road
Atglen, PA 19310
Phone: (610) 593-1777; Fax: (610) 593-2002
E-mail: Info@schifferbooks.com

For the largest selection of fine reference books on this and related subjects, please visit our web site at
www.schifferbooks.com
We are always looking for people to write books on new and related subjects. If you have an idea for a book please contact us at the above address.

This book may be purchased from the publisher.
Include $3.95 for shipping.
Please try your bookstore first.
You may write for a free catalog.

In Europe, Schiffer books are distributed by
Bushwood Books
6 Marksbury Ave.
Kew Gardens
Surrey TW9 4JF England
Phone: 44 (0) 20 8392-8585; Fax: 44 (0) 20 8392-9876
E-mail: info@bushwoodbooks.co.uk
Website: www.bushwoodbooks.co.uk
Free postage in the U.K., Europe; air mail at cost.

Contents

THE FAMOUS BARNEGAT LIGHT

On the Boardwalk, at Beach Haven, N. J.

Acknowledgments

There are a number of people who I would personally like to thank. In some way or other, over the course of time, these people have helped me in ways great and small. For that I am deeply indebted. First and foremost, to my partner Ray Tombaugh I owe thanks for first sharing the magic of Long Beach Island with me, and then continuing to share it with me through the highs and lows life deals us. To my dear friend Jeanette Lloyd, I thank you for being comforting and affirming, while at the same time giving me a kick in the seat of the pants when I need it. To David Lloyd, who at the drop of a hat, and in the aftermath of a blizzard, helped me out on one of the worst days I have ever had. To Kathe Van Harte, the most creative person I know, and someone who has enjoyed my postcards as much as I do. Your friendship, inspiration, and company made a very cold and lonely winter on Long Beach Island a very special time for me. Thank you also to my dear friend Kathryn Ayres for taking the time to voluntarily proofread this volume for me. To Bob Stewart, thanks for allowing me to probe your memory and for answering my questions. Thanks also go to Diane Stevens for providing me with information on Benjamin Archer and his Barnegat City.

To the many other friends on Long Beach Island who have been there when we needed them; Joanna & Brett Madden, Jake Madden, Rich and Karen Vaughn of Bistro 14, Susie Anderson who is a real life-saver, Steve & Debra Farber; people who truly know the meaning of being a good neighbor, June MacFarlane & Gus Doyle, John Harquist who is the most reliable guy on Long Beach Island, Jeff Lopez, Walt McCollum who is the island's best Plumber and HVAC guy ever, John & Gretchen Coyle who gave us much needed words of encouragement and support, Bill Burris, a stand up kind of guy who was willing to help someone he barely even knew, and to Deb Whitcraft, for her support and encouragement.

Lastly, a thank you to our friends and neighbors on Second Street, and thereabouts, in Beach Haven, who opened your doors to us and made life there just a little more enjoyable. Polly Fullmer and her late husband Bob, Bobby Fullmer, Wallace & Esther Ruoff, Rosemary Ruoff, and Sally, Mary, & Elizabeth Dwyer.

THE FLEET, BEACH HAVEN, N. J.

Introduction

The beach towns and barrier islands that collectively make up the Jersey Shore are unique places. Over time each of them has developed its own well-defined character and persona and for much of their century-and-a-half histories, these places have come to represent different things to different people. To me, they are much like the members of a family.

Cape May will always be the fussy Grandmother of the shore family, while Ocean Grove is its strict, starch-collared Father. Ocean City, naturally, is everyone's teetotaling Aunt. Atlantic City is the painted-up Sister who marries well, but somehow you just know it won't last, while Asbury Park is definitely the Redneck Cousin of the bunch.

And then there is Long Beach Island. LBI, as those in the know fondly refer to her, is like the Younger Sister of the family. She is delicate and fragile, a natural beauty with a glow that outshines all others. In the minds of those who know and love her, she remains forever young and forever beautiful.

She lies six miles at sea, and eighteen miles long, stretching like a nubile beauty from Barnegat Light at the northern tip to Holgate at her southern end. This graceful spit of sand off the coast of New Jersey has an allure unlike any of her rivals. Her siren song, played on a never ending loop, has lured people to her beaches and her towns for the better part of two centuries. And every summer, year after year, generation after generation, they continue to heed her call.

Ask anybody who has experienced the delights of Long Beach Island just what it is that continues to attract them and you will surely get a host of answers. Eventually, though, it always comes down to the sand, the sun, the quality of the experience, and this mystical, yet indefinable something that was planted within them the first time they crossed the bay, smelled the salt marshes and sea air, and placed their feet firmly on the island. It is something that, once planted within you, never lets go. And it is something that time can never diminish.

It has been this way since people first started coming to LBI and it remains that way today. Her people are fiercely loyal, almost to the point of looking down their noses at the rest of the beach resorts. Many would rather skip their vacation all together than to suffer the indignity of having to spend it anywhere else at the shore. And on the other hand, the closet fear amongst all who partake of this island Shangri-La is that our communal secret will be leaked out, everyone else will discover her, and then all will be lost. Such are the foibles of the connoisseurs of Long Beach Island.

This depth of emotion felt for the place is not something new. A letter in my collection, penned in July of 1878, most likely by a guest at the Parry House in Beach Haven at the island's southern end, expresses many of the same sentiments those of us feel today with regards to the powerful spell that the island casts upon us. The writer states, "To tell the truth my heart always sinks when the time comes for leaving (for) home." She continues by writing of the joy experienced by her child as he tells her to "tell Aunt Emmie that the ocean is more beautiful today than it ever was in its life. There are big high waves all over it all the time. I wish you could see his eyes while he is telling about it." Anyone who loves the island can read these words today and still understand completely every one of the emotions behind them. They are feelings that remain timeless.

The proprietary feeling that each of us has towards the island doesn't just end at the sand and the surf. It also includes the island's history. For many of us her history is our history, and we have one man to thank for making that history come to life, John Bailey Lloyd. His articles, books, and Monday night lectures throughout the summer, every summer, filled our minds with visions of the Baldwin and Engleside Hotels, of Captain Bond and the Barnegat Lighthouse, sneakboxes, yacht clubs, and of course every one of the island's legendary watering holes.

His lectures were always delivered to a sold-out crowd, packed into a sweltering room, and produced with only a slide projector and screen, yet he had the knack to keep us entertained, and to keep us coming back for more. Through his writings and his lectures I developed an interest in the history of Long Beach Island. And through this shared interest in her history we developed a friendship. Every year I would look forward to my week's vacation on LBI to see what lecture JBL (as he was fondly referred to by those who knew him) would be delivering. I was fortunate to be able to hear a great many of them over the years, and none of his deliveries ever disappointed. He was truly THE authority on the island's history and yet remained one of the humblest and most approachable men I have ever known.

Once bitten by the history bug, as a longtime collector of antique postcards and vintage images, it was only natural that I should direct my attentions to the Island of Long Beach and begin collecting her history too. My partner Ray had actually been the one to introduce me to the Island and together we dove into collecting the island's history. His family had been coming to the island since the early 1940s and to them it had become like a second home, complete with all the aforementioned emotions.

Together we scoured flea markets and postcard shows looking for these elusive scraps of paper. Trust me when I tell you that they are not easy to find. Interestingly, dealers will either have no images of the island, or they will have a bunch of them. There is no in between. Much of this, I feel, has to do with the fact that those special people, who in the early days were drawn to LBI and began to vacation there religiously, sent cards back to the same people year after year. Resultantly a cache of cards that were sent over time from the island will turn up from one person or estate. As a collector, it can be frustrating as dealer after dealer tells you they have nothing for you, but the payoff when you hit that one dealer who has just discovered a horde of LBI images more than offsets the frustration.

We shared with John each new discovery and he, in turn, regaled us with tales of what each card and photo represented. It was always an enjoyable time when we sat back and started discussing the history of the island. Many a happy summer afternoon was spent on the shady vine-covered porch of his Third Street home with post-cards spread before us and drinks in hand.

A continuing mantra throughout John's lectures, writings, and our personal conversations was how the face of Long Beach Island was constantly changing, and not always for the better. The grand hotels that had once been the backbone of island tourism were long gone. Victorian cottages and twenties bungalows were falling one by one as skyrocketing land values, and basic supply and demand, devalued the island's architectural heritage. Longtime businesses from bath houses, to stores, to miniature golf courses were being gobbled up by greedy developers whose only source of taste was in their mouths. Driven forward by the almighty dollar, they were intent on re-making the island into their ticky-tacky vision of what they thought the place should be, regardless of what anyone else thought. It then became more important than ever to remember, and to accumulate, the island's past before it was all swept away completely.

Eventually Ray and I bought and restored one of the historic cottages in Beach Haven, where we became neighbors with John and his wife Jeanette. Instead of spending one week a year on the island, we began to spend every summer weekend there, along with many of the spring and fall weekends too. Sharing new finds became much easier then, as did, with the growth of the Internet, the ability to scan and send them back and forth via e-mail. And the ability to collect using e-Bay at any hour of the day or night helped our collection to grow substantially.

Alas, after nearly twenty years of collecting, helping to save an important part of Beach Haven's history from the wrecking ball, and a cross-country move from the shores of the Atlantic to the shores of the Pacific, we have decided to break up this collection that has grown to over 700 postcards, photographs, and related souvenirs. John Bailey Lloyd's untimely death in July of 2003 and the sale of our much-loved Beach Haven Victorian took much of the wind from the sails of this collection. It is time that others are allowed to add these images to their collections with the same enthusiasm and excitement with which we first discovered them. The creation of this book results in a permanent reminder of the cards and images from our collection that can now be shared and enjoyed by all who view it.

It is a collection a long time in the making and yet one that I've never felt was complete. There are many great images out there that we know eluded us, yet for each one of those, we have discovered something else equally as interesting that we added to our collection. For those with an interest in island history, and in the postcards and images that chronicled it, it is never too late to start collecting. Just as with any collectible, there will always be those items valued beyond your reach. You will see by the prices included in this volume that the rarest of LBI images are only for the serious collector, or the novice with very deep pockets. The nice part of this is that for every one of those rare images and cards, there are plenty more that are, with some searching, available and reasonably priced for even the entry-level collector with scant resources. All you've got to do is get out there and start looking.

And our fondest hope is that seeing these images and reading about the island's history will awaken the same sense of urgency in you that John Bailey Lloyd's lectures and writings awakened in us. We hope it will force you up out of your beach chair and out from beneath your umbrella, and make you start thinking about just what it is that makes LBI so special to you, and, just how easily it could all be lost. Ask yourself what disappeared this past winter while you were away if you want to get really motivated, and then get out there and do something to prevent it from happening again. We can't replace what's already gone. We can collect postcards and historic images to remind us of that, but everything else is a part of your, and our, collective experience. It is part of what has made, and continues to make, Long Beach Island such a special place. ***Cherish it. Value it. And work to protect it now and forever.***

A Value Guide to Long Beach Island Postcards & Photographs

The pricing of postcards can be a very subjective thing. What one dealer sees in a postcard and prices accordingly for, another may completely gloss over. Educated postcard dealers are learning where to price these cards and bargains are getting harder to find. Yet recently at a postcard show I came across a spectacular Beach Haven postcard priced at a quarter! There are still bargains to be had.

With that said, there are a few general rules of thumb to keep in mind when "postcarding." Long Beach Island was never as heavily visited as places like Atlantic City or Asbury Park. So it is safe to say that not nearly as many postcards were produced of the island, sold on the island, or sent from the island. Resultantly, when you factor in their throwaway nature, it means that there are fewer of these cards to be found today than postcards of Atlantic City or Asbury Park. Their scarcity dramatically affects their price.

There are new people who are beginning to collect postcards of Long Beach Island all the time. That means that in addition to their scarcity, the demand is constantly rising. These newer collectors are not aware that ten years ago many of these cards sold for as little as three to five dollars. They are seeing the prices that postcard dealers are pricing their cards at, accepting that those prices are the going rate for these cards, and purchasing them at prices that make longtime collectors weak in the knees.

And then there is the elephant in the room; the thing that has been fueling all of this – online auctions. In one respect they are great in that they bring to the surface all kinds of material from all over the world. The downside is that the savviest dealers and collectors are the ones that are utilizing online auctions, which in turn makes for very competitive bidding for some very scarce items, with the fallout being that the prices realized in these auctions are what many other dealers then use to price their new inventory.

The prices that I have quoted in this book are prices that, in many cases, have actually come from online auction results. Some may look at these prices and consider them aberrations or extremely overinflated. What I would say to that is that for any auction to have risen to the pricing level that these did, it takes **two** bidders. That means that more than one person was willing to pay just about that same price for that same postcard. And in the case of many of these auctions, there were multiple bidders whose final bids were all hovering very near to the final sales price. It was only the most extreme auction price results that had just two bidders.

The fact of the matter remains that the best and scarcest items in any category of collectible will always demand the best prices. And in the case of postcards from Long Beach Island you have the perfect congruence of scarcity, increasing demand, and online accessibility, all intersecting to set prices at levels that just a few years ago would have been unimaginable. My suggestion is this; use these prices as a guide to know what the top value is on any of these cards. If you are able to purchase copies of these cards anywhere beneath what this value guide states, then you have done well.

As for the pricing of photographs and other memorabilia from the island, that is not as well defined. A great majority of the people who collect postcards are only into postcards. It is generally a smaller subset of the larger group of postcard collectors that are also into photographs and memorabilia. While most photographs are truly one-of-a-kind items, and both are very scarce, the prices quoted within this book are fair prices. There just isn't as large a group of people that are interested in these items, or are actively seeking them out. But those that do are happy to pay almost any price for this material.

Chapter 1
Where It All Began

It seems appropriate enough to begin any book that combines the history and images of Long Beach Island, where the island actually began, with the sea, the sand, and the surf. Long Beach Island is just one of the many barrier islands that lie off the eastern coast of the United States. She was created eons ago by the erosion of coastal beaches, and was augmented by the ever-surging ebb and flow of the tides. The island grew up from out of the sea through the same action that creates the much smaller sand bars that develop off her beaches today.

As the island developed, bodies of water became isolated behind her with inlets that allowed access to them. Many mistakenly refer to the entire body of water that was created behind LBI as Barnegat Bay, however, that is only correct in the broadest sense. It is actually three separate and distinct bodies of water. At the southern end of the Island is found Little Egg Harbor. In the center, where the causeway crosses, is the Manahawkin Bay, and to the north, stretching well beyond the tip of Long Beach Island, is what is correctly identified as Barnegat Bay.

Over time, through the continual action of the tides, LBI developed into the island that we have come to know today. As the underpinnings of the island were being formed, the forces of nature also combined upon her surface to create row upon row of giant coastal sand dunes. These dunes were nature's way of protecting what she had created from the onslaught of the waves during harsh coastal storms. As long as they remained untouched, the island of Long Beach had no reason to fear for her survival.

Early Morning on the Beach, Beach Haven, N.J. c. 1910. $3-5

OFF BEACH HAVEN, N.J.

Off Beach Haven, N.J. c. 1905. $6-8

Sunrise Over Ocean, Long Beach Island, N. J.

Sunrise Over Ocean, Long Beach Island, N.J. c. 1940. On the reverse: Here all the magic of seashore charm is captured at the first blush of dawn over the clear blue waters of the Atlantic Ocean. Long Beach Island comprises six seashore resorts: Beach Haven, Long Beach, Ship Bottom, Surf City, Harvey Cedars and Barnegat City. $3-5

Sand Dunes   Beach Haven, N. J.

Sand Dunes, Beach Haven, N.J. c. 1930. At one time the dunes on Long Beach Island were massive and were two and three rows deep. It is said that they were so high that you could get lost within them when you could no longer hear the ocean or the town noises to give you direction. Children who grew up on the island would climb them and then toboggan down as though they were snow covered hills somewhere in the country. $8-10

"Where the Sea makes in"   Beach Haven, N. J.

"Where the Sea makes in" Beach Haven, N.J. c. 1930. When the communities like Beach Haven began to develop on the island, one of the first actions taken was to level the dunes. This was done partly to provide fill for low-lying areas, but also to give that much-wanted, unimpeded ocean view to people building hotels and cottages in those towns. Little did these people realize that the dunes were nature's way of protecting the island. $4-6

Sand Dunes, Beach Haven, N.J. c. 1913. It would take coastal storms, like the Hurricane of 1944 and the March Northeaster of 1962, and a growing sense of environmentalism, to begin to make people realize the damage that they had brought upon themselves by eradicating the dunes. $4-6

Sand Dunes on Long Beach Island, N.J. c. 1937. In the 1970s, with the birth of the environmental movement, real action was taken to stabilize what dunes were left, and to help to build new ones in an environmentally correct fashion. The planting of dune grass, with roots that went several feet deep down into the dunes, has helped to re-grow the dunes in an effort to try to rebuild the island's natural system of defense. Today the dunes of Long Beach Island are protected just as though they were members of an endangered species. $3-6

Long Beach Island, N.J. c. 1975. $2-4

Chapter 2
Beach Haven, The Queen City of Long Beach Island

From the beginning, Long Beach Island has been a destination. Her first visitors are generally thought to have been the members of various native tribes. These included the Lenni Lenapes who were drawn to the island and bay by its abundant natural resources. In those days the bay was full of fish, the skies were black with migratory fowl, and the beaches relinquished a bountiful harvest of shellfish, all of which provided sustenance for these native peoples.

It was these same abundant resources that brought the first non-native settlers to the island. As early as 1690, whalers had begun to take up residence on the island in the vicinity of what is now Surf City. But it was the sport fishing and hunting, so readily available on Long Beach Island that would bring together the men who would become the key players in the island's future.

Captain Thomas Bond's Long Beach House, located just south of what is today Beach Haven, became a destination for wealthy sportsmen from Philadelphia. It was there, at Bond's, that Archelaus Pharo, a Tuckerton resident who was instrumental in the creation of the Tuckerton Railroad, became acquainted with many of the men who would later become summer citizens of his soon-to-be-created Beach Haven.

Sources indicate that Pharo would annually take his wife to Bond's at the height of hay fever season. Here she would find seasonal relief from her misery. The restorative qualities of Long Beach Island were obvious. The island in those days was a pretty barren place. Native plants like bayberry and beach plum grew in abundance; however, the plants and weeds that were the cause of summer hay fever were not to be found there. Being so far out to sea, and with a prevailing ocean breeze gently purifying the air for most of the summer, the allergens of the mainland were kept far enough at bay so as to provide tremendous relief to those who suffered.

Pharo recognized the value in the recuperative qualities of the island. And as a good businessman, with a railroad that could bring people directly to the shores of Little Egg Harbor, and a steamboat that could transport excursionists across the bay on the final leg of their journey, he set out to create a new resort community on the Island.

It is said that one of Pharos's daughters came up with the name Beach Haven for the new community he was planning. There was a strong push by Dr. A. A. Willits to add an extra "e" and name it Beach Heaven, most likely because of its otherworldly charms; however, this idea did not prevail. And thusly, in 1873, the Tuckerton and Long Beach Building & Land Improvement Association was chartered.

Through his association with the Tuckerton Railroad, and also his connections from Bond's Long Beach House, Archelaus Pharo began a long association with the firm of Burnham, Parry, Williams & Company, better know as the Baldwin Locomotive Works of Philadelphia, Pennsylvania. Because of their mutual business interests, the men behind this company took an active interest in the creation of Beach Haven. Many of them were veterans of Bond's and were already familiar with the allure of LBI. So it was no surprise that a number of them were initial subscribers to the Land Improvement Association's lot sales.

According to family legend, Pharo told the surveyors to find the highest spot of ground in this newly laid out town and that is where he chose to build the first two cottages. These two homes, Louella Cottage, which he had built for himself, and Sheepshead Cottage, built for Dr. Albert Smith of Philadelphia, another of the veterans of Bond's Long Beach House, were designed as duplicates of one another. They welcomed their first guests during the summer of 1874 and still stand side by side today between Atlantic and Beach Avenues on Second Street in Beach Haven.

No seashore resort could be considered complete without the addition of a luxury hotel and Beach Haven was not to be outdone on that count. In 1874 Charles Parry, another veteran of Bond's Hotel and one of the principals of the Baldwin Locomotive Works, set about constructing the Parry House, a four-story Victorian seaside hotel, complete with a mansard roof and a rooftop cupola. It too welcomed its first guests during the summer of 1874. Located on the north side of Centre Street between Beach and Atlantic Avenues, it appears to have been the epitome of style with its broad verandahs. Each room had an ocean view.

The nucleus of the original town plan centered on the area from Amber Street on the south, to Third Street on the north, and from Atlantic Avenue to Bay Avenue. And it was within this area that the majority of the Land Improvement Association's early lots were sold. Two additional avenues to the east appear on early maps. They are Seaside Avenue, which would today run through the middle of the beach and dunes, and Ocean Avenue, which would be just off the beach, out in the surf. Needless to say, neither of these streets was ever realized.

Another peculiarity that appears on the 1874 map of Beach Haven is that Beach Avenue was originally laid out quite a ways further east of its present location. Originally it would have run directly between the Smith and Pharo cottages. In 1876, a new map was drafted to encompass the streets as far south as Ocean Street so that additional building lots could be created. At that time, Beach Avenue was fixed at its current location and adjustments were made to the lots that had already been sold to accommodate this change. Since that time, except for a few minor changes, the community known as Beach Haven has remained pretty much as she was originally planned by her creators.

Greetings from Beach Haven.
c. 1949. $8-10

Promotional Booklet,
Beach Haven New Jersey
and the Lure of the Sea.
c. 1929. $300

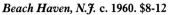

Beach Haven, N.J. c. 1960. $8-12

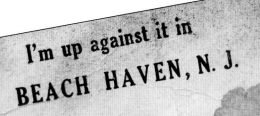

Beach Haven, N.J. c. 1965. $3-5

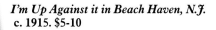

I'm Up Against it in Beach Haven, N.J.
c. 1915. $5-10

Come and try this in
Beach Haven, N. J.

Greetings from Beach Haven, N.J. c. 1948. $4-6

Come and Try This in Beach Haven, N.J. c. 1915. Taking their cue from risqué French postcards, some stores in Beach Haven produced and sold these naughty comic cards. It is possible that they may have been too much for the staid little town since these versions are the only copies of any of them that have ever resurfaced. $5-10

Greetings from Beach Haven, N.J. c. 1950. $3-6

Greetings from Beach Haven, N.J. c. 1955. $2-3

Greetings from Beach Haven, N.J. c. 1968. $2-3

The Beach

Relief from hay fever may have been the initial draw to Beach Haven, but it was her wide, glorious, wind-swept beaches, with sand as fine as sugar, that has kept people coming back for over one hundred and thirty years. Surf bathing, as it was then called, was a popular attraction at each of the communities on Long Beach Island. Nowhere was it more so than in Beach Haven, where each of the large hotels had their own bath houses in which the beachgoer could change into, and out of, their heavy woolen bathing suits and all of the trappings that accompanied them.

In the early days, there was a strict protocol about when and where you could be seen in a bathing suit. They were meant for use on the beach, and only on the beach. It was considered pretty much taboo to cross Atlantic Avenue in one, let alone to dare think of entering into any of the resort's hotels while dressed in one. Today those customs are all but forgotten as people have become much more relaxed about their bodies and their appearance while vacationing at the shore. Hang-ups are checked at the causeway and fun is all that matters.

Sand Dunes and old Wreck on Beach, Beach Haven, N.J. c. 1908. In the early days, wrecks like these dotted the beaches of Long Beach Island. Charles Edgar Nash, in his 1936 edition of *The Lure of Long Beach*, estimates that to that date upwards of 500 ships have perished off the beaches of Long Beach Island. $40-50

Summer Life, Beach Haven, N.J. c. 1910. "Dear John, I wish you were here to play with me. I like the ocean & have lots of fun in the water. With Love - Henry". $15-20

On the Beach, Beach Haven, N.J. c. 1905. $20-25

On the Beach, Beach Haven, N. J.

A SUMMER AFTERNOON, BEACH HAVEN, N.J.

A Summer Afternoon, Beach Haven, N.J. c. 1908. $20-25

Uncaptioned Real Photo Postcard by Photographer Louis P. Selden, Surf Bathing at the Engleside Hotel. c. 1913. Robert Engle installed a float out in the surf in front of his hotel that swimmers could make their way out to and also dive from. That float is what you see on this postcard. $50-75

The Beach, Beach Haven,
N.J. c. 1922. $15-20

Kiddies on the Beach   Beach Haven, N. J.

Kiddies on the Beach, Beach Haven, N.J. c. 1930.
While adults love the beach, those that get true
enjoyment from it are really the children. Armed
with sand buckets and shovels they dig into the
beach to build castles and sand forts with energy
that adults can only wish they had. The next few
images highlight the children's joy during beach
time. $15-20

Photograph, Child on
Beach, Beach Haven,
N.J. c. 1930. $10-20

Photograph, Children at Play Beach Haven, N.J. c. 1930. $20-30

Fort Defiance, Beach Haven, N.J. c. 1909. **This photo was taken by Robert Engle of the Engleside Hotel. It has also appeared with the title "Awaiting the Spanish Armada," which would probably date it to the time of the Spanish-American War. This elaborate sand castle is replete with flag and sewer pipe cannons. $30-40**

On the Sand at Beach Haven, N.J. c. 1925. $15-20

Photograph, Mother and Daughter in front of Engleside Hotel. c. 1930. $10-12

Bathing Beach, Beach Haven, N.J. c. 1925. $30-40

On the Beach, Beach Haven, N.J. c. 1925. I find it amazing that stylishly dressed women thought nothing of sitting on the beach, complete with heels, just so they could read a book! $30-40

Photograph, Men and Car at Beach, Beach Haven. c. 1930. This photograph was taken along the Centre Street plank walks to the beach. The cottage in the rear on left is the Taggart Cottage, one of the Seven Sisters Cottages, located at the corner of Second Street and Atlantic Avenue. The building on the right is the rear of the refreshment stand on the boardwalk at Second Street. $20-25

Beach Scene, Beach Haven, N.J.
c. 1925. $25-30

Beach Scene, Beach Haven, N. J.

23

Photograph, On the Beach, Beach Haven. c. 1928. $10-15

On the Beach, Beach Haven, N.J. c. 1935. This card, and the one that follows, are two of the most beautiful cards from Beach Haven. These images were hand-tinted by people with watercolors. Can you imagine the human effort that went into painting these postcards, one by one, only to have them thrown away after they had been used? Yet look at the delicacy with which each of these images was tinted. It seems almost inconceivable to us today that someone could have once taken the time to do this. $50-60

In the Surf, Beach Haven, N.J. c. 1937. "Dear Jennie, Have had a fine week resting, picking shells, paddling and going to the movies. Saw *Silent Bravery, Hollywood Cowboy, Behind the Headlines* and expect to see on Saturday, *I Met Him in Paris.* Helen." $50-60

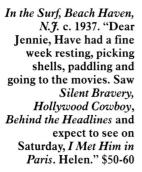

Photograph, Family on Beach in Front of Boardwalk and Engleside Hotel. c. 1930. $30

On the Beach, Beach Haven, N.J. c. 1920. "This is where we went swimming this a.m. Russell & Mary enjoyed it immensely and want to go again. We wound up with a bath in the ocean. It's fine. Wish you could enjoy the coolness of it all." $15-20

Beach Scene, Beach Haven, N.J. c. 1938. "We're on vacation here on an island. We can barely see the mainland." $15-20

Photograph, Girl and Dog and Boardwalk, Beach Haven. c. 1928. $10-15

Beach Scene, Beach Haven, N.J. c. 1935. $40-50

Beach Scene, Beach Haven, N. J.

Photograph, Lifeguard and Girls on Beach, Beach Haven. c. 1930. $20

Photograph, Woman on Beach, Beach Haven. c. 1935. $5-10

Surf Bathing at Beach Haven, N.J. c. 1938. On the reverse: The warm sand, sea and sunshine of magic Long Beach Island reaches a peak of health on the beachfront of Beach Haven, the "Queen Resort" of magic Long Beach Island, N.J. $6-12

On the Beach at Beach Haven, N.J. c. 1944. $5-10

Beach Scene, from Boardwalk, Beach Haven, N.J. c. 1940. $6-12

Sun Bathers on the Beach, at Beach Haven, N.J. c. 1944. "We had excitement here to-day, saw two navy planes crash in mid-air & come down very near here, in fact the one motor fell out here in the bay. I suppose this week will go very fast. Hilda, Lew & Boys." $8-12

Beach Haven, N.J. c. 1963. $3-6

Photograph, Man and Dogs, Dunes, Beach Haven. c. 1960. The young man in the photograph is Ben Creamer of Allentown, Pa. and his two pet spaniels. This photo was taken on the dunes at the foot of Amber Street by his father in September of 1960. $10-15

Surfing at Beach Haven, N.J.
c. 1967. Surfing really began
to take off in the 1960s on
Long Beach Island. Places like
Koseff's Surf Shop and The
Ron Jon Surf Shop helped to
establish LBI as the East Coast
capital of surfing. $5-10

*Ocean Bathing, Beach Haven,
N.J.* c. 1962. "Today we are
here to see the results of the
awful storm. I'd hate to have
been here!" $3-6

Greetings from Beach Haven, N.J. c. 1965. $4-8

The Beach Haven Beach Patrol

The act of saving those in peril on the sea has a long and storied history on Long Beach Island. It began formally with the first House of Refuge that was constructed in Harvey Cedars in the 1800s. Through the Life Saving Stations that replaced them, to the United States Coast Guard, and right on up to the current Beach Patrols in each of the shore communities, looking out for one's fellow man while he either sails upon the ocean's surface or frolics about in her rolling surf, is not a job to be taken lightly. People's lives are at stake and vigilance is the word of the day.

In the early days, the primary focus of the Life Saving Stations was to rescue the unfortunate victims of shipwrecks off the Jersey coast. There were many such incidents. With each heroic rescue of passengers and crew, the need for a vital Life Saving Service became further strengthened. Eventually the Life Saving Service was merged with the Revenue Cutter Service to create what we know today as the United States Coast Guard.

With the birth of Beach Haven and the construction of her large hotels, surf bathing became a popular pastime. For a great many of these visitors it was likely the first time that they had ever taken a dip in the Atlantic. Lines were strung out into the ocean so that the less adventurous bathers could safely maintain their footing. Yet there are daredevils in every crowd and it became quite clear to the management of the hotels that looking out for the welfare of their guests was important. Nothing would kill business like bathing accidents. The Engleside Hotel advertised that a lifeboat and life saving apparatus was always on hand during bathing hours.

By the 1920s each one of the shore communities had active, organized beach patrols that worked their beaches. The Beach Haven Beach Patrol's operations were run from a Red Cross pavilion located on the Beach Haven boardwalk.

The role of a lifeguard is hard work. Entrusted with the lives of all who play on their beach, and with hundreds of people to keep an eye on simultaneously, it is not for the faint of heart. Just as they were way back then, lifeguards remain the masters of all that they survey. In addition, they are icons of beach culture. They are respected, admired, and yes, even adored by those they protect, as should be readily evident in the following selection of images.

The Life Boat afloat   At Beach Haven, N. J.   71-2

The Life Boat Afloat At Beach Haven, N.J. c. 1906. **This postcard shows a typical vessel used by the Life Saving Service to rescue people in danger on the open water. $40-50**

On the Beach at Beach Haven, N. J.

On the Beach at Beach Haven, N.J. c. 1938. By the 1920s, the shore patrol duties were pretty much centered on the individual community's beach patrol. In most of the shore towns, the beach patrols, or lifeguards as they were commonly known, sat raised up in elevated chairs, such as the one depicted here, so that they could easily scan the horizon for those in peril. $3-6

The Life Boat, Not Coast Guards, But May Be, Long Beach, N J.

The Life Boat, Not Coast Guards, But May Be, Long Beach, N.J. c. 1916. $15-25

Photograph, Unidentified Member of the Beach Haven Beach Patrol (BHBP). c. 1930. All of these photographs of the BHBP come from the photograph albums of the young man in this picture. He remains unidentified, just as do his fellow beach patrol members. It would appear that he served a number of seasons in the BHBP as he appears to age in the photographs. This photo was taken at a patrol stand on the beach at the end of Second Street. $30-40

Photograph, Unidentified Members of the Beach Haven Beach Patrol (BHBP). c. 1930. Here the BHBP patrol the beach in front of the Engleside Hotel. $20-30

Photograph, Lifeguards and Children, Morning Calisthenics, Beach Haven, N.J. c. 1930. This series of three photographs documents what was an every morning beach activity sometime in the late 1920s to early 1930s. A Beach Havenite has told me that each morning the lifeguards would meet with the children of town, and those vacationing there, and they would perform a series of exercises with them. One of these photos was even used in a promotional booklet that the town sent out to prospective tourists. $60-80

Photograph, Lifeguards and Children, Morning Calisthenics, Beach Haven, N.J. c. 1930. $60-80

Photograph, Lifeguards and Children, Morning Calisthenics, Beach Haven, N.J. c. 1930. $60-80

Photograph, Lifeguard Posing with Beachgoers, Beach Haven, N.J. c. 1930. $20-30

Photograph, Lifeguard Posing with Beachgoers, Beach Haven, N.J. c. 1930. $20-30

Photograph, Lifeguard Posing with Beachgoers, Beach Haven, N.J. c. 1930. $20-30

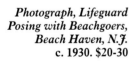

Photograph, Lifeguard Posing with Beachgoers, Beach Haven, N.J. c. 1930. $20-30

The Boardwalk

The New Jersey Shore and the boardwalk are two terms that for most people go hand in hand. You almost can't even think of the one without immediately thinking of the other, and for good reason. They've been around a long time. Cape May is given credit with creating the first crude boardwalk in 1868. The much more famous Atlantic City boardwalk followed two years later in 1870. Beach Haven would follow suit, but it would take almost thirty years to do it.

In 1896, Robert B. Engle proposed construction of a small-scale boardwalk, only eight feet wide, which would connect his Engleside Hotel with the Baldwin Hotel four blocks to the south. Ostensibly this was done in an effort to allow hotel patrons to stroll the sandy beaches without dragging sand back into the hotels. In reality it was more likely that Engle saw the amount of business that an attraction like a boardwalk brought to places like Atlantic City, and he too wanted a piece of this action.

The original Beach Haven boardwalk was laid out flat upon the sand. The enormous dunes that had once graced the beaches of LBI had, for the most part, been obliterated by then in the name of ocean views and cheap landfill. So it was an easy construction job. Its success was immediate and in short order Engle began proposing construction of an even larger and more elaborate boardwalk.

The second boardwalk was constructed in 1898. This structure was raised up off the sand and was twelve feet wide. Kerosene lamps on poles lined the boardwalk so that evening strolls could be enjoyed. Eventually it would stretch for over a half a mile, from Sixth Street on the north to Marine Street on the south. Throughout its almost twenty-year existence it remained, on purpose, a simple affair. The only businesses to adjoin it were the Engleside and Baldwin bath houses.

To understand the mindset of the times in choosing to keep the boardwalk a simple affair, one just needs to read a page from George Somerville in his 1914 volume, *The Lure of Long Beach.* He discussed this very subject when he spoke up in defense of the tranquility that hard working vacationers sought on their visits to LBI, and railed against the honky-tonk "qualities" of many New Jersey shore resorts. "True seashore rest is the antithesis of the fatigue and weariness produced by man's or woman's participation in the toil and stress of his or her own particular phase of the world's work. And the truly restful bit of seashore is that where the flippant, tantalizing and fictitious so-called 'amusements' are absent. Ancient merry-go-rounds with wheezy organs are out of place beside the majestic solitudes of old ocean; screeching vaudeville 'queens' should be voiceless within the sound of the breakers' roar, and claptrap 'shows' and mendicant 'fakirs' are out of place where men and women gather for rest from year-round work and city 'attractions'."

Shortly after he wrote this, though, things began to change. People started to think differently about what kind of development they wanted to see on the island. With the completion in 1914 of the new auto bridge connecting the island to the mainland, people began streaming into Beach Haven. There were big thoughts about the future of the island and many large projects were undertaken in the town during that period. By 1916, it was felt that Beach Haven needed an even larger boardwalk and thus a walk twenty feet wide was constructed, replacing the earlier structure. It stretched from Holyoke Avenue at its south end to Seventh Street at its north.

Again the new boardwalk was an immediate success. This time around, with thoughts of progress and growth populating everyone's brains, it was decided to allow the construction of businesses along the boardwalk facing the ocean. Lots were sold off and a number of small commercial buildings were constructed. Blueprints and drawings still exist for the construction of a large theater on the boardwalk proposed by Beach Haven's Osborne Realty. For reasons that remain unknown, it was never built.

The idea of a boardwalk with commercial enterprises just never quite took off in Beach Haven the way it did in other shore communities. There was additional construction though. At the end of the 1920s a large skee ball arcade was erected on the boardwalk at Centre Street. In the end, a boardwalk lined with businesses was an idea that was only marginally successful. This was probably for the best given the eventual fate of both the boardwalk and those businesses.

The Great Atlantic Hurricane of 1944, which came roaring up the eastern seaboard of the United States in September of that year, brought death, destruction, and ruination to much of the Jersey shore, Beach Haven included. One of her victims was the Beach Haven boardwalk. Witnesses reported that it broke up into sections that went sailing bayward, through the streets of Beach Haven, on storm tossed waves. Eventually the lumber that remained was salvaged and sold to Atlantic City to make repairs to her boardwalk since the war was still on and supplies were scarce.

It was discussed for a great while afterward whether the boardwalk should be rebuilt. However, in the intervening years since its construction, there had been a bit of a power shift in Beach Haven, with the year-round residents taking over control of the community from the summer dwellers and hotel companies that had originally established and controlled it.

Their priorities were oftentimes very different, and their feelings toward the tourists and part-time residents, and toward what they wanted, were not often favorable. Most likely it was a combination of economics, given that this was a country still reeling from the effects of a great depression and a world war, and, the desire by many to see a certain "element" removed from the beaches of LBI that boardwalks tended to attract, that nixed its rebuilding. With the destruction of the boardwalk, Beach Haven's attempts to be an Atlantic City-style resort came to an end.

These images of the Beach Haven boardwalk that follow are among the scarcest of all postcards and images from Long Beach Island. They had to have been produced in enormous quantities at the time, yet where are they today? They are almost non-existent. Those lucky enough to find any of them rarely find them reasonably priced. My guess is that nostalgia for this long-lost landmark is what keeps people hanging onto these postcards and photographs as treasured mementos of Beach Haven's glorious past. As each year passes it becomes increasingly difficult to find anyone who can honestly say that they once strode the Beach Haven boardwalk.

The Board Walk and Beach, Beach Haven, N.J. c. 1905. This early view shows Beach Haven's second boardwalk, taken just south of the Engleside bathhouses. $35-40

Boardwalk Scene, Beachhaven, N.J. c. 1908. This postcard was sent to Miss Elisabeth Cyptors, Model Poultry Farm, East Aurora, NY. The message on the reverse just said, "Grandma was fortunate to catch one crab." $80-90

Beach Scene, Beach Haven,
N.J. c. 1905. $15-20

Beach Scene, Beach Haven. N. J.

Sand Dunes, Beach Haven, N. J.

Sand Dunes, Beach Haven, N.J.
c. 1911. Although it offers but the
briefest glimpse of the boardwalk,
this is an early card showing Beach
Haven's second boardwalk. $15-20

Copyright 1905 by the Rotograph Co.
A 6350 Bath Houses and Boardwalk, Beachhaven, N. J.

Bath Houses and Boardwalk, Beach Haven, N.J. c. 1908. These are the Baldwin Hotel's
Bath Houses located on the beach directly in front of the hotel. The amazing thing about
this image is the artistic license taken by the publisher of the card. This shows Beach
Haven's second boardwalk, which was only twelve feet wide, yet on this image it appears
to be double that width. $50-60

Bathing Strand, Beach Haven, N.J. c. 1922. $75-85

Photograph, On the Boardwalk in Front of the Baldwin Bath House. c. 1928. This image shows Beach Haven native George Lee on the right, and an unidentified gentleman, sitting on a bench in front of the Baldwin Hotel's Bath House. Lee's Mother at one time managed and ran the bathhouse concession. $30-40

Aerial View of Beach Haven, N.J. c. 1930. This view shows much of the length of Beach Haven's second boardwalk. It was built in 1916 and survived until 1944. $40-50

07   Boardwalk, Beach Haven, N. J.

Boardwalk, Beach Haven, N.J. c. 1925. S. K. Simon of New York City published a huge series of postcards of Long Beach Island that dates to approximately 1925. They are mostly hand-tinted with watercolor, and they capture the island and its landmarks in the 1920s almost better than anyone else was able to. The cards produced by Simon are highly desirable additions to any LBI collection. $75-85

2043   Beach & Boardwalk, Beach Haven, N. J.

Beach & Boardwalk, Beach Haven, N.J. c. 1925. This view shows the boardwalk at the foot of Engleside Avenue. The use of ramps to access the boardwalk was a novel approach that allowed people of all ages and infirmities to easily make the climb. It predates by decades the accessibility issues of today. $30-40

Photograph, Family on Beach below Boardwalk. c. 1930. $100-115

Beach View, Beach Haven, N.J. c. 1925. In addition to ramps for access to the boardwalk, there were also plank walks that attached it to all the businesses and structures that were located adjacent to it. In addition, plank walks extended off the boardwalk that stretched across the sand all the way to Atlantic Avenue. This postcard shows some of those walks attached to the structures that were located in front of the Engleside Hotel. $65-75

09   Beach View, Beach Haven, N. J.

Photograph, Boy on Beach and Boardwalk. c. 1932. This photograph was taken very near to the beach end of Second Street, looking south towards the boardwalk pavilion and the Engleside Hotel. $75-100.

Boardwalk and Pavilion, Beach Haven, N. J.

Boardwalk and Pavilion, Beach Haven, N.J. c. 1925. After the third boardwalk was built in 1916, lots were sold and structures and businesses began to be built along it. This municipal pavilion, designed by the Philadelphia architectural firm of Savery & Scheetz, housed public restrooms and was also a cool shady place to rest and watch the ocean. $40-60

On the Boardwalk, Beach Haven, N.J. c. 1925. Looking north on the boardwalk from Amber Street, the building in the center of the image, and located in front of the Engleside Hotel, was the Maison Mae dress shop, a high-end ladies' apparel store. In the distance is the municipal pavilion. $25-30

On the Boardwalk, Beach Haven, N. J.

Bathing Scene, Beach Haven, N.J. c. 1935. Probably the most well known of all vintage images of Beach Haven, this view, taken from out in the surf, looks up at the Beach Haven Boardwalk. The Maison Mae dress shop is directly in the center and to the right of it is the iconic tower of the Engleside Hotel. $60-75

On the Beach at Beach Haven, N.J. c. 1925. Taken from the foot of Engleside Avenue, this view looks south towards the Engleside Bath House and the Maison Mae dress shop. $40-50

1237   Come and See Shop and Bath Houses, Beach Haven, N. J.

Come and See Shop and Bath Houses,
Beach Haven, N.J. c. 1926. Within a
short time of opening, the Maison
Mae was renamed the Come & See
Shop. Presumably they sold the
same type of merchandise. $100-125

Photograph, Boardwalk Stores, Beach Haven,
N.J. c. 1930. These two buildings, located on the
boardwalk just north of the ocean end of Second
Street, were built around 1920. The building on
the left was a hot dog and refreshment stand.
The building on the right was Madame Lilly's
Tea Room, owned by Lilly Schlingloff. Madame Lilly's survived the Hurricane of 1944
but was demolished sometime afterwards.
$60-80

Photograph, Unidentified Employee
Standing Outside Madame Lilly's
Tea Room, Beach Haven Boardwalk.
c. 1930. Whether this is actually
Madame Lilly Schlingloff, or just
one of her tearoom employees, is not
known. $20-30

45

Studio Photograph, Beach Haven, N.J. c. 1915. Getting your photo taken on vacation in the days before everyone had pocket cameras was a special thing to do. Most places of amusement had a photo gallery and Beach Haven was no exception. The Beach Haven photo gallery was located in a building adjacent to the Engleside Bath House. Two photographers are known to have worked in Beach Haven. One was Louis P. Selden and the other was a photographer who stamped his photos Sawyer & Co. $5-10

Studio Photograph, Beach Haven, N.J. c. 1908. Not all studio photos are stamped identifying them as being from Beach Haven. One sure way to identify an uncredited studio photo is to compare the painted backdrop and the furniture the people are posed on with a known example from the studio. This photo, identified as Sawyer & Co., is especially collectible because it shows a child, but more importantly because it shows what is today an antique sand pail. Collectors of old toys love vintage photos that show the toys they collect. $50-60

Studio Photograph, Beach Haven, N.J. c. 1915. The message on another card says, "Selden and Co. said that they have mailed the photos. In case you do not receive them let him know and he will send others. My father is here. The maid left, I may have to go home. Affectionately, Alice." $5-10

Studio Photograph, Beach Haven, N.J. c. 1906. Compare the backdrop and the chair in this photo with the backdrop and chair in the photo with the child. This card is not identified as to the photographer, but it is clearly a Beach Haven studio shot. $5-10.

01   Beach View, Beach Haven, N. J.

Beach View, Beach Haven, N.J. c. 1925. Taken in
front of the Engleside Bath House, this image
shows another pavilion just to the right that
was located on the boardwalk. This pavilion
probably belonged to the Engleside Hotel. It
also gives a good idea of the amount of open
space that there was between the boardwalk and
Atlantic Avenue. The houses in the background
are on Atlantic Avenue between Engleside
Avenue and Centre Street. $100-115

Photograph, In the Engleside Pavilion.
c. 1933. This photograph of George
Lee and the young lady that he had
married was taken in the Engleside
pavilion and is dated July 1, 1933, on
the reverse. $25-30

Photograph, Engleside Pavilion after Northeaster. c. 1935. It is thought that this photograph shows the destruction wreaked upon a portion of the Beach Haven boardwalk by the northeaster of November 1935, the same storm that washed out the railroad trestle to the island. $35-40

Boardwalk, North from The Engleside. Beach Haven, N. J.

Boardwalk, North from The Engleside, Beach Haven, N.J. c. 1926. $80-100

Boardwalk and Beach. Beach Haven, N. J.

Boardwalk and Beach, Beach Haven, N.J. c. 1928. $120

Boardwalk and Beach, Beach Haven, N.J.

Boardwalk and Beach,
Beach Haven, N.J.
c. 1927. $85-100

The Boardwalk. Beach Haven, N. J.

The Boardwalk, Beach Haven,
N.J. c. 1930. $30-40

Photograph, Lady on Boardwalk, Beach Haven,
N.J. c. 1922. **This photograph was taken on the**
boardwalk at the end of Second Street. The
Benner Cottage is behind this lady, on the left,
at the corner of Centre Street and Atlantic
Avenue. On the right is the Shonders Cottage
at the corner of Second Street and Atlantic
Avenue. Today it is the Heather House Bed &
Breakfast. $20-30

Boardwalk, Beach Haven, N.J.
c. 1925. This image was taken on the boardwalk at the Baldwin Hotel bathhouses. The Beach Haven Fishing Pier is behind the women on the left. $20-30

Boardwalk and Beach, Beach Haven, N.J.
c. 1938. Taken very close to the same spot as the previous postcard, in the intervening years, Downing's Playland Skee-Ball Arcade had been built at the foot of Centre Street. Playland would be destroyed in the Hurricane of 1944 along with the boardwalk. $45-50

Boardwalk and Beach, "Six-Miles-At-Sea" Beach Haven, N.J. **c. 1930. $45-55**

BOARDWALK. BEACH HAVEN, N. J.   20

Boardwalk, Beach Haven, N.J. c. 1942. "Hi Kids, Your Home and we're gone. Money goes so fast down here. I'd like to know where it goes." $15-25

Photograph, Lifeguard and Girls on the Boardwalk. c. 1932. $20

On the Boardwalk, Beach Haven, N.J. c. 1945. Sent to Mrs. Lester Weiner, Bethlehem, Pa. "Dear Ruth, This is a beautiful spot and the children just love it. Everything is perfect & am eating like a horse – the food is so wonderful, Regards to all. Don." $20-25

On the Boardwalk. at Beach Haven, N. J.

Boardwalk and Beach, Looking South, Beach Haven, Long Beach, N.J. c. 1940. Standing on the boardwalk in front of Madame Lilly's Tea Room and looking south, this would have been your view around 1940. $50-60

Beach Haven, N.J. c. 1962. Taken on the beach at the end of Centre Street, and looking north, your eye follows the path where the Beach Haven boardwalk once stood. Very few structures on the boardwalk survived the Hurricane of 1944. The refreshment stand at the end of Second Street did. It continued to operate for a great many years but was eventually demolished. $3-6

The Hotels of Beach Haven

From the time that Archelaus Pharo first laid out his new resort community, through today, Beach Haven has never been without a hotel or lodging establishment to serve the visitors who come each year to partake of what the town has to offer. Her grand hotels helped to set the standard for luxury and hospitality at the Jersey shore, each year serving thousands of guests during the summer season. The Parry House was the first of these great sand castles by the sea.

Charles T. Parry was the driving force behind its construction and it was in his honor that the hotel was named. Parry, one of the owners of the Baldwin Locomotive Works in Philadelphia, lavished money and attention on this structure in an attempt to make it one of the Jersey shore's premier destinations. It far outdistanced Captain Bond's old Long Beach House in both size and luxury. When it opened in June of 1874, it signaled that Beach Haven was rightfully ready to take its place amongst all of the other seashore resorts.

Sadly, the history of the Parry House was to be short-lived. With her rooms filled almost to capacity, she caught fire and burned to the ground on the night of August 10, 1881. Fortunately not a single life was lost in the conflagration. In 1886 the land upon which the Parry House once sat was subdivided into building lots. By 1896, all of the lots had been sold and new seashore cottages had replaced the ruins of Beach Haven's first hotel.

Postal Cover, Parry House, Beach Haven, N.J. sent July 23, 1879. Very little material exists from the Parry House as it was in existence for less than eight years, and then it was only open part of the year. This cover from the Parry House refers to Beach Haven as "The New Ocean Resort, Island of Long Beach, Five Miles at Sea." The really important thing about this cover is the fact that they were already marketing themselves as being five miles out at sea. Prior to the discovery of this cover, it was thought that the Six-Miles-At-Sea slogan of Beach Haven, and of LBI, was a 1920s marketing creation. $200

Letter, Parry House, Beach Haven, N.J. sent July 20, 1878, to London, England and forwarded on to Christiana, Denmark. The person who wrote this letter was most likely staying at the Parry House Hotel, as she mentions, "We had services here in the parlor this morning. An English Episcopal clergyman officiated, but somehow a hotel church does not seem like Sunday." There were strong Episcopalian ties to the Parry House, including the Episcopal cleric who alerted the guests the night of the fire that destroyed it, which is what leads us to believe that this is where this letter was written and sent from. $175

The Engleside Hotel

Robert Barclay Engle arrived in Beach Haven in 1874 to manage the newly built Parry House for Charles Parry and his investors. Engle, a Quaker from Mount Holly, quickly realized the potential for profit that existed in this newly created resort. With that thought in mind he recruited his cousin Samuel T. Engle and together these two men created a hostelry whose name would become forever synonymous with Beach Haven: The Engleside Hotel.

The Engles hired the well-known Quaker architect, Addison Hutton of Philadelphia, to design a hotel for them that would rival the Parry House in both size and luxury. By 1875, Hutton was considered one of the principal architects of Philadelphia, and associating his name in the development of an enterprise of this nature, especially one that catered to the Philadelphia crowd, was a stroke of genius on their part. The Hutton firm and its successors would continue to do design work in Beach Haven well into the 1920s.

Surprisingly, the design that they got from Hutton, while attractive, looked remarkably similar to the Parry House. A large structure that sat perpendicular to the beach afforded every room an ocean view. The roof of the building was capped with a large viewing platform, much like that on the Parry House. Construction of the hotel on a lot that was bounded by South and Amber Streets and Atlantic and Beach Avenues was completed in time to welcome its first guests for the summer season of 1876.

People today are often confused when they see early images of the Engleside Hotel. The original design of the structure was basically a long rectangle with the center section slightly recessed from either of its ends. Long balconies stretched across the end facing the ocean and the hotel's primary façade and main entrance were oriented to South Street.

What is missing from these views is its distinctive tower with arcaded porches and conical roof, capped by a lantern. This fanciful piece of construction would not be added to the hotel until 1890 when a major renovation and expansion was done to the then almost fifteen-year-old hotel. The addition of this tower created a new and iconic focal point for the structure. From that point on, and until its demise, all official views of the Engleside would focus on the tower, with the hotel stretching off in the distance, rather than on its South Street entrance.

In 1901, upon the death of Robert B. Engle, the hotel passed into the hands of Robert Fry Engle, son of its creator and founder. Robert Engle the son was an accomplished photographer whose images of the island adorned the hotel and graced many of its brochures, advertisements, and postcards. His would be the hand that would guide the hotel until its eventual demise in the 1940s.

Engraving, Beach Haven, N.J., Engleside, R. B. & S. T. Engle, Prop. c. 1878. **This engraving from** *Woolman and Rose's Atlas of the New Jersey Coast* **shows the original Engleside Hotel before the addition of the tower structure. $30-50**

The Engleside Tennis Club Courts, Beach Haven, N.J. c. 1910. This is probably my favorite postcard of the Engleside Hotel. It appears here in the prime of its existence, colored as close to what sources say was the hotel's actual paint scheme. $10-15.

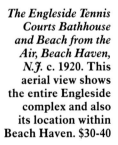

The Engleside Tennis Courts Bathhouse and Beach from the Air, Beach Haven, N.J. c. 1920. This aerial view shows the entire Engleside complex and also its location within Beach Haven. $30-40

Promotional Booklet, Engleside and Beach Haven (24 pages). c. 1900. The Engles, both father and son, were master promoters of their hotel and of their community. This glossy booklet was sent out on request. Within its pages it extolled the virtues of the hotel, the pollen-free air, the beach, and a hundred other benefits of visiting Beach Haven. $100-150

Sample Page, Promotional Booklet, Engleside and Beach Haven (24 pages). c. 1900.

The Engleside Hotel will accommodate about 350 guests, and is remarkable for its light, cool, airy effect and its roomy exchange, corridors and porches. It is but a stone's throw from the ocean, and the nearest one to the sea in the town, and has an unobstructed view of it, save for its pavilion and bathing houses.

So many hotels have back rooms whose outlook is objectionable. The Engleside stands endwise to the sea, and EVERY ROOM in it has a view of the ocean

At the ocean end of the hotel is a large Assembly Room, with great windows open to the sea breeze on three sides, in which an orchestra gives daily morning concerts and dance music in the evening.

The hotel has the modern necessities of elevator, gas, electric bells, and hot sea water baths.

The Hotel

Every Room has an Ocean View

Assembly Room

The Dining Room

Sample Page, Promotional Booklet, Engleside and Beach Haven (24 pages). c. 1900.

*The Engleside,
Beach Haven, N.J.*
c. 1906. $10-15

*The Engleside Motor Bus,
Beach Haven, N.J.* c. 1905. In
the early days a street car line
had been set up to get people
from the wharf, and later
from the railroad station, to
Beach Haven's hotels. Robert
F. Engle purchased this
motorbus as a replacement
for the tediously slow horse-
drawn streetcar. This was
the first motorized means of
conveyance in Beach Haven.
$50-75

*The Engleside, Beach
Haven, N.J.* c. 1910.
Postcard printers, most
of which were located
in Germany before the
Great War, were often
very imaginative in
their use of color when
printing postcards, as
evidenced by the red roof
on the hotel. $6-10

Postal Cover, Engleside Hotel, Beach Haven, N.J. c. 1898. $15-20

The Engleside, Beach Haven, N.J. c. 1932. **For some reason very few postcards exist that show the Engleside full on from the south. This is one of the rare exceptions. $20-25**

The Engleside   Beach Haven, N. J.

Photograph, Engleside Hotel and Tower. c. 1938. **This photograph shows the portion of the Engleside Hotel that was added in the expansion of 1890. $15-20**

Engleside Hotel, Beach Haven, N.J. c. 1905. $12-15

Engleside Hotel, Beach Haven, N.J.

Promotional Booklet, Engleside Hotel. c. 1920. $40-60

The Engleside, Beach Haven, N. J.

The Engleside Hotel, Beach Haven, N.J. c. 1910. "Dear Anna, Came down today. Lots nicer than Atlantic City." $15-20

The Engleside and Beach Haven

The Engleside, Beach Haven, N.J. c. 1925. "Dear Della & Jimmie, I am spending a week down here. It is grand – fishing & bathing every day. At night I can see down to Atlantic City." $30-40

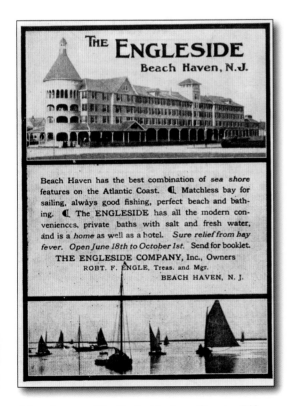

THE ENGLESIDE
Beach Haven, N.J.

Beach Haven has the best combination of *sea shore* features on the Atlantic Coast. ⁋ Matchless bay for sailing, always good fishing, perfect beach and bathing. ⁋ The ENGLESIDE has all the modern conveniences, private baths with salt and fresh water, and is a *home* as well as a hotel. *Sure relief from hay fever. Open June 18th to October 1st.* Send for booklet.

THE ENGLESIDE COMPANY, Inc., Owners
ROBT. F. ENGLE, Treas. and Mgr.
BEACH HAVEN, N. J.

Advertisement, The Engleside, from Country Life Magazine. c. 1906. $5-10

The Engleside, Beach Haven, N.J. c. 1930. $10-20

The Engleside from the Tennis Courts, Beach Haven, N.J. c. 1925. By the 1920s, Beach Haven had become a center of tennis playing. Both the Engleside and the Baldwin Hotels had multiple courts, and they were attracting big name players to them. The most famous visitor was Big Bill Tilden. $40-60

Engleside Hotel, Beach Haven, N.J. c. 1935. By the 1930s, the Engleside Hotel was in trouble. The kind of traveling that it had been built for, where families decamped for an entire month at a time was a thing of the past. In addition, the building of houses all over the island converted many of LBI's hotel guests into vacation homeowners. $15-20

Engleside Tennis Courts, Beach Haven, N.J. c. 1932. Just beyond the tennis courts are the Engleside bath houses. $10-15

Menu, The Engleside, Beach Haven, New Jersey. **August 21, 1938.**

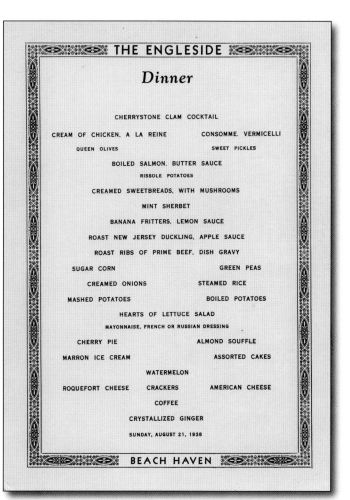

Dinner

CHERRYSTONE CLAM COCKTAIL

CREAM OF CHICKEN, A LA REINE   CONSOMME, VERMICELLI

QUEEN OLIVES   SWEET PICKLES

BOILED SALMON, BUTTER SAUCE

RISSOLE POTATOES

CREAMED SWEETBREADS, WITH MUSHROOMS

MINT SHERBET

BANANA FRITTERS, LEMON SAUCE

ROAST NEW JERSEY DUCKLING, APPLE SAUCE

ROAST RIBS OF PRIME BEEF, DISH GRAVY

SUGAR CORN   GREEN PEAS

CREAMED ONIONS   STEAMED RICE

MASHED POTATOES   BOILED POTATOES

HEARTS OF LETTUCE SALAD

MAYONNAISE, FRENCH OR RUSSIAN DRESSING

CHERRY PIE   ALMOND SOUFFLE

MARRON ICE CREAM   ASSORTED CAKES

WATERMELON

ROQUEFORT CHEESE   CRACKERS   AMERICAN CHEESE

COFFEE

CRYSTALLIZED GINGER

SUNDAY, AUGUST 21, 1938

BEACH HAVEN

Menu, The Engleside, Beach Haven, New Jersey. **August 21, 1938. Engle was deeply in debt by the time this menu was printed; yet it did not stop him from putting out the most lavish of spreads for his guests, let alone printing up a fancy menu each and every day. $50-60**

Engleside Hotel, Beach Haven, N.J. **c. 1938. The owner of this postcard has just penned on the reverse "Memories!" $6-12**

AERIAL VIEW. BEACH HAVEN. N. J.

137636

Aerial View, Beach Haven, N.J. c. 1939. The summer season of 1940 would be the last for the old hotel. The contents were auctioned off by the Philadelphia auction house, Samuel T. Freeman & Co., and the hotel was put up for sale for back taxes. When no one stepped forward to buy the old place, the Borough of Beach Haven reluctantly took the property in lieu of the taxes that were owed. In 1943 the hotel was dismantled and salvaged piece by piece as there was a war on and building materials had become scarce. Today Bicentennial Park is all that remains of the old Engleside Hotel. $10-15

Arriving at Beach Haven

In the early days, travel to Long Beach Island was an arduous affair. Travelers changed from river steamers, trains, stagecoaches, and then boats, one after another, as they made their way, primarily from Philadelphia, to her sandy shores. With the creation of the Tuckerton Railroad, access improved dramatically, yet the trip to LBI could still be a long, drawn-out affair.

And if that wasn't arduous enough, most that were traveling were not coming alone. With them came spouses, children, nannies, servants, pets, suitcases, hatboxes, trunks, and many times an entire household of goods to furnish their summer cottage. It's a wonder they ever made it. The final leg of the trip was made on a paddle wheel steamer to either Beach Haven on the south, or to Barnegat City on the island's north end.

In 1885, the Pennsylvania Railroad was enticed to build a spur line onto Long Beach Island by real estate investors with ready capital to help cover the costs. A low trestle-type bridge was constructed across the marshes with a drawbridge that would allow for boats to get past this new connection. Construction on the project was finally completed in 1886. For the first time communities all along the length of the island were connected with one another, and with the outside world, by passenger rail service.

Christened the Manahwakin & Long Beach Railroad, its arrival on the island would usher in a new era of development in much the same way that the completion of the auto bridge would thirty years later. Substantial stations were built in each of the island's major communities with smaller structures serving the newly developing areas. It was to these stations that travelers arrived on the final leg of their journey, hot, sweaty, and most times covered in soot.

Train Time, Beach Haven, N.J. c. 1906. This was the Pennsylvania Railroad's Beach Haven station, which was located on the bay end of Third Street. It was a quite substantial structure built to serve the thousands of visitors that came to Beach Haven annually. When the trains stopped coming to Beach Haven, this building was converted into a private residence. It was torn down to make way for new houses in 1999. $15-20

Rapid Transit at Beach Haven, N.J.

Rapid Transit at Beach Haven, N.J.
c. 1906. Horse-drawn streetcars picked
up arrivals at the station in Beach
Haven and then wended their way into
the heart of town to deliver visitors to
hotels and cottages. $30-40

Beach Haven, N.J.
c. 1910. In addition
to the town's horse
car line, the Baldwin
Hotel had its own
horse-drawn streetcar.
This image shows that
horse car heading east
on Pearl Street at the
intersection of Beach
Avenue. This, and the
two cards that follow,
are all very rare and are
almost impossible to find.
$130-150

Beach Haven, N. J.

The New Hotel Baldwin.

Hotel Acme, Beach Haven, N.J. c. 1910.
This view shows the Baldwin horse car
heading west on Pearl Street alongside
the Baldwin Hotel. It is thought that the
title of this card is an error, as the Hotel
Acme was on the bay at the end of Dock
Road. The cottage in the background was
historically known as Sunbeam Cottage.
$120-140

Hotel Acme, Beach Haven, N. J.

Rapid Transit in Beach Haven.   Published by A. J. Durand.

Rapid Transit in Beach Haven, N.J. c. 1910. With the arrival of automobiles to the island, the old horsecar lines were abandoned in favor of motorized vehicles. $60-80

The Baldwin Hotel

After fire destroyed the Parry House in 1881, Charles Parry and his group of investors re-grouped and decided to build anew. Instead of rebuilding on the same site, a choice plot of land was purchased between Atlantic and Beach Avenues, and between Pearl and Marine Streets. It was on this site in 1883 that their new creation, designed by Wilson Brothers & Company of Philadelphia, arose.

Named the Arlington Inn, this fabulous confection of Victorian architecture, laid out in an L-shaped design, rose a full four stories high. Its surface was rife with bays and brackets, balconies, porches, lightning rods, weathervanes, and turrets. Its most memorable design elements, though, were the Moorish cupolas that crowned the ends and main corner of the great hotel.

About a year after its construction, a large addition was built adjoining the hotel on the west. It was at this point in time that the hotel was rechristened as the New Baldwin Hotel. This was done in honor of Mathias Baldwin and his Baldwin Locomotive Works, the source of wealth and prominence for many of Beach Haven's most esteemed summer citizens.

The Baldwin Hotel would thrive for a great many years. It provided an alternative to the family-oriented, soberingly dry experience of the Engleside Hotel. The Baldwin appealed to the vacationer with a spring in his step and a thirst to be quenched. The two hotels had very different clientele, yet each independently succeeded and prospered.

Charles Parry died in 1887, and by 1910 the Baldwin was being run by his grandson Mercer Baird, a spoiled, gluttonous man with no self control. He spent money that he didn't have on the hotel and on his own lavish entertainments. A modernization campaign, aimed at capturing the throngs of people that would arrive with the opening of the causeway auto bridge and the new boulevard, ran him deep into financial debt. Eventually, though, it all caught up with him. By 1916 the Baldwin had passed from family hands. And thus began its long downward spiral.

To say that its final years were all bad would be untrue. The roaring twenties breathed much new life into the old hotel. New owners would modernize it further but bit-by-bit what had made it so beautiful began to disappear. The architectural ornament was stripped piece by piece from its façade, its porches were enclosed, then partially removed, and then, finally, its Moorish cupolas were truncated and capped.

A fire in August of 1947 would be just a foretaste of what was to come. By 1960 this once-grand seashore Victorian hotel was nothing but an ugly, outdated relic waiting for disaster to strike – and it did. On September 24th of that year, a huge fire would level the entire hotel in a matter of hours, leaving nothing but a smoldering heap of brick and ash where once had stood the magnificent Hotel Baldwin.

New Hotel Baldwin, Beach Haven, New Jersey. **c. 1916. While the Baldwin was a big hotel, this artist's rendering of the place makes it look as though it stretched on for blocks. $20-40**

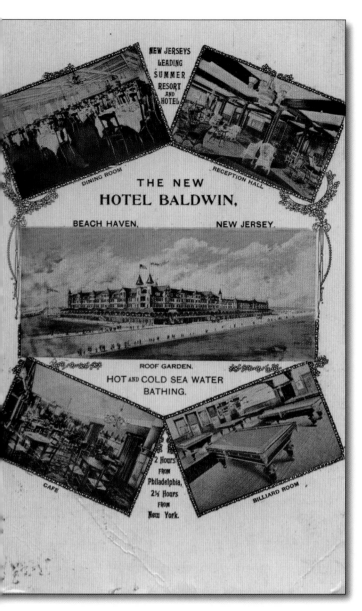

THE NEW
HOTEL BALDWIN,

BEACH HAVEN,   NEW JERSEY.

HOT AND COLD SEA WATER
BATHING.

Souvenir China Vase, The New Hotel Baldwin, Beach Haven, N.J. c. 1915. Souvenir China from Beach Haven is extremely rare. In twenty years of collecting, I have only ever seen three pieces of it. This miniature vase was made by Millar China in Germany and retailed by Haidee Nakamura in his Japanese Novelty Store on the boardwalk. $100-125

The New Hotel Baldwin. c. 1912. This is a very special card in that these are some of the only interior views known to exist of the Baldwin Hotel. Shown on this postcard are the Dining Room, the Reception Hall, The Café, and the Billiard Room. The Baldwin was quite an elaborate place. No expense had been spared on its appointments and it showed. $150

Mark, Souvenir China of Hotel Baldwin.

Hotel Baldwin, Beach Haven, N.J. c. 1910. $15-20

Souvenir of Hotel Baldwin, Beach Haven, N.J. c. 1905. $10-15

Souvenir of Hotel Baldwin, Beach Haven, N.J. c. 1906. $10-15

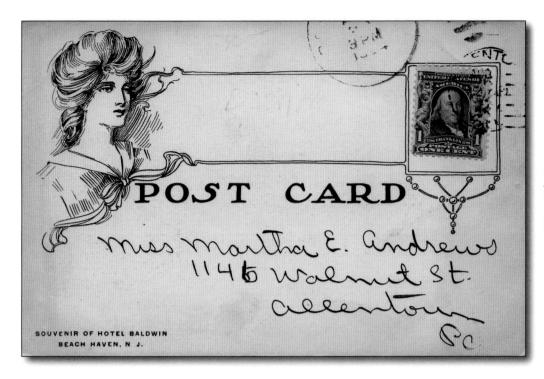

Souvenir of Hotel Baldwin, Beach Haven, N.J. c. 1904. Even the backs of postcards were made attractive in those days. $10-15

SOUVENIR OF HOTEL BALDWIN
BEACH HAVEN, N.J.

POST CARD

*Miss Martha E. Andrews
1146 Walnut St.
Allentown
Pa.*

Baldwin Hotel, Beach Haven, N.J. c.1908. The Baldwin did not stay open as long as the Engleside. One postcard sender wrote on September 9, 1913, that the "Hotel closed today, moved over to the Engleside." $12-15

Baldwin Hotel, Beach Haven, N.J.

TENNIS COURTS
HOTEL BALDWIN,
BEACH HAVEN, N.J.

Tennis Courts, Hotel Baldwin, Beach Haven, N.J. c.1908. Tennis was just as big a deal at the Baldwin as it was at the Engleside. This great image shows the tennis courts, which were located just in front of the hotel. The elevated porch of the Baldwin made a fantastic grandstand to watch the tennis matches. This postcard is also great in that it gives you a close-up view of the façade of the Baldwin Hotel. Its surfaces were covered in fancy patterned shingles, and Victorian gingerbread covered many surfaces. $20-30

Restaurant China Platter, Hotel Baldwin, Beach Haven, New Jersey. c. 1920. One of the most highly sought pieces of memorabilia from the Baldwin Hotel is a piece of china from the hotel's Dining Room. Very few pieces seem to exist and those that do turn up can command hefty prices. $500-800

The New Hotel Baldwin, Beach Haven, N.J. c. 1910. $25-35

Souvenir Paperweight, New Hotel Baldwin, Beach Haven, N.J. c. 1910. Souvenir items from a vacation fondly remembered are a staple of any trip. The same was true a century ago when this glass paperweight depicting the Hotel Baldwin was sold as a souvenir somewhere in Beach Haven. $70-90

1253   Baldwin Hotel, Beach Haven, N. J.

Baldwin Hotel, Beach Haven, N.J. c. 1925. This rather quirky view shows the back end of the hotel along Beach Avenue. Because this was not a traditional view of the hotel, it makes it a bit harder to find today. $30-50

Hotel Baldwin, Beach Haven, N.J. c. 1930. $18-25

Hotel Baldwin, Beach Haven, N.J. c. 1938. $8-12

HOTEL BALDWIN — BEACH HAVEN, NEW JERSEY

Aerial View, Beach Haven, N.J. c. 1939. By the 1930s, miniature golf had overtaken tennis in popularity in Beach Haven. The Baldwin Hotel put up what was probably the first miniature golf course on the island on top of the old hotel tennis courts. $12-16

137637

THE BALDWIN HOTEL, BEACH HAVEN, N. J.

The Baldwin Hotel, Beach Haven, N.J. c. 1935. In this view of the hotel, you can see just a small portion of the miniature golf course with people playing upon it. $6-12

Aerial View Baldwin Hotel and Beach Haven, N. J.

Aerial View Baldwin Hotel and Beach Haven, N.J. c. 1945. This view of the Baldwin, and of Beach Haven, documents the changes that had come about by the end of World War II. Missing from this image are the Engleside Hotel, demolished in 1943 to pay for back taxes, and the boardwalk, destroyed in the Hurricane of 1944. $8-12

81019

Hotel Baldwin at night, Beach Haven, N.J. c. 1940. This postcard also appears in a matching daytime view. $2-4

HOTEL BALDWIN FIRE, AUG. 9 1947 - BEACH HAVEN, N.J.

Hotel Baldwin Fire, Aug. 9, 1947 –Beach Haven, N.J. c. 1947. This extremely rare, one-of-a-kind real photo postcard, most likely snapped by an onlooker to the blaze, shows the events that unfolded on the afternoon of August 9, 1947, when a smoky fire routed guests from the Hotel Baldwin. A great number of oceanfront rooms, along with the hotel's dining room, were heavily damaged by the blaze. $150-250

Baldwin Hotel, Beach Haven, N. J.

Baldwin Hotel, Beach Haven, N.J. c. 1949. This postcard helps to convey the downward spiral that the hotel had started into by the 1950s. Porches have started to be removed along with other decorative elements, including the Moorish cupolas. $2-4

Aerial View of Beach Haven, New Jersey. c. 1960. By 1960, Beach Haven, along with all of its counterparts at the Jersey Shore, was beginning to feel its age. With travelers jetting off to exotic locales instead of loading up the car and heading to the shore, a backward slide began. Nobody wanted these Victorian cottages, or worse yet, wanted to stay in hotels without the latest conveniences. The Baldwin Hotel suffered right along with everyone else. In this view, the streets are virtually empty, and the development land grab that would redefine the island within the next 30 years had not yet begun. $5-8

Baldwin Hotel, Beach Haven, N.J. c. 1960. This has got to be the ugliest postcard ever produced of the Baldwin Hotel; however, by the time 1960 rolled around, it really was a rather decrepit, ugly place. The last ounce of charm that it had was long gone, and no amount of artistry could doctor up its image. When it burned to the ground in September of 1960, it really brought the curtain down on Victorian Beach Haven. That curtain would not be raised again for another twenty-five years, when people would once again begin to appreciate the history and beauty of Beach Haven's past and begin to work diligently to protect it. $3-6

Baldwin Hotel, Beach Haven, N. J.

The Small Hotels and Guest Houses of Beach Haven

In addition to her three grand hotels – the Parry House, The Engleside, and the Baldwin Hotel – Beach Haven has been, and continues to be, home to a great many other small hotels, guest houses, and Bed & Breakfast establishments. Each has its own unique history and place in the community. A number of these establishments have been around for a century or more. The last half-century has seen the addition of motels to Beach Haven, many of which have now been on the scene almost as long as were her classic hotels. For new generations of vacationers, they have become the classics.

The St. Rita Hotel, Beach Haven, N.J. c. 1928. The beginnings of the St. Rita Hotel are not entirely clear. The structure was probably built around 1876, when the Tuckerton & Long Beach Land Improvement Association's records show the lot upon which it sits as having been sold. Sources indicate that the first owner was a family named Dease, and that when the husband and primary breadwinner of the family took ill, Mrs. Dease turned the place into the St. Rita hotel as a means of keeping the family's head above the water financially. $150

Business Card, Hotel St. Rita, Beach Haven, N.J. E. A. Dease, Prop. c. 1928. It is said that Mrs. Dease prayed to St. Rita, whom she considered to be her patron saint, and that it is from this that the hotel received its name. St. Rita, among other things, is the patron saint of desperate, seemingly impossible causes and situations, and also the patron saint of sick people and widows. $50-60

St. Rita Hotel, Beach Haven, N.J., Open All Year. c. 1945. Today the St. Rita Hotel is one of the oldest, continuously operating hotels at the Jersey Shore. It has only ever been run by three families. The current innkeeper of the St. Rita is Marie Coates. $50-65

OCEAN HOUSE
Center Street   Beach Haven, N. J.   11635

Ocean House, Beach Haven, N.J. c. 1930. The Ocean House was another of Beach Haven's earliest lodging places. Located on the north side of Centre Street, between Beach and Bay Avenues. It was a huge, rambling, Victorian structure that extended back very deeply onto its lot. The old hotel served guests for close to a century before it was torn down. Today Julia's of Savannah, a beautiful neo-Victorian bed & breakfast, sits on the site of the old Ocean House. $90

Beach Haven House, Beach Haven, N. J.

Beach Haven House, Beach Haven, N.J. c. 1920. The Beach Haven House was built by Lloyd Jones, the former owner of Bond's Long Beach House. Jones bought the very first parcel of land sold in the new town of Beach Haven and built his hotel, which was patterned to look like Bond's, at the very foot of Mud Hen Creek at the corner of Bay Avenue and Centre Street. It was, along with the Parry House, one of the first operating hotels in town. In 1938, the old building was pushed back to the rear of the property so that its then-owner, Richard Lamb, could build a new restaurant facing Bay Avenue. It was demolished in 1967. $50-60

865 THE BILTMORE, Beach Haven, N. J.

The Biltmore, Beach Haven, N.J. c. 1927. This was another of the small guesthouses in Beach Haven that catered to the vacationer without the resources to stay at one of the big hotels. Located on the west side of Bay Avenue between Dock Road and Second Street, today the building still stands, though somewhat enlarged, as a retail store. $225

The Magnolia, Center Street between Beach and Bay Ave., Beach Haven, N.J. c. 1935. This classic Victorian served visitors to Beach Haven for over one hundred years. It has recently been turned into a private residence. $70

The Magnolia
Center St. between Beach and Bay Ave.
Beach Haven, N. J.   11643

The St. Louis House, Bay & Norwood Avenues, Beach Haven, N.J. c. 1930. The concept of bed & breakfast lodging began when people started opening their private homes to paying guests, inviting them in and making them feel like part of the family. Places like the St. Louis House, which today is a private residence, though not called a B&B, were the progenitors of this new style of American lodging. Original photograph from which the postcard was made, $40-60.

The St. Louis House, Bay and Norwood Aves.
Beach Haven, New Jersey

31075

Fairview Court, Fairview Avenue, Beach Haven, N.J. c. 1945. Fairview Court was an updated version of the guest cabin concept that had become popular with the arrival of the automobile. Instead of cabins, there were apartments described on the reverse of the card as "modern, restricted apartments" with "two to four rooms" and they were soundproofed. $25-35

Bayview Manor Hotel, Beach Haven, N.J. c. 1956. Located on the bay at Coral Street & West Avenue, the Bayview was a motel with a liquor license that allowed the owners to also run a restaurant and bar. $3-6

Bayview Manor Hotel, Beach Haven, N.J. c. 1956. On the reverse: Visit our cocktail bar, with lounge adjoining, where the finest drinks are served and friendliness prevails. Overlooking picturesque Little Egg Harbor Bay. Open to the public. $3-6

Dining Room, Bayview Manor Hotel, Beach Haven, N.J. c. 1956. On the reverse: Gracious dining, each table with a view of Little Egg Harbor Bay. Dinners, ala carte, served to the gourmet's taste. Open to the Public. $3-6

The Engleside, 30 East Engleside Avenue, Beach Haven, New Jersey. c. 1966. The Engleside name returned to Beach Haven with the building of the new Engleside Motel, just feet away from where the old Engleside Hotel had stood. Today the Engleside continues to welcome guests with the same sense of hospitality that its predecessor was known for. $5-10

Sea Shell Motel and Club, On the Beach at Center Avenue, Beach Haven, N.J. c. 1964. **Across Engleside Avenue from the Engleside Motel is the Sea Shell Motel. It described itself as having "the convenience and economy of a motel plus all the comfort and luxury of a resort hotel." Today the "Shell" continues to draw visitors to LBI. $3-5**

Coral Seas Motel, On the Ocean at Coral Street, Beach Haven, New Jersey. **c. 1968. On reverse: 38 luxuriously furnished units, each with individually controlled air conditioning and electric heat, large modern coffee shop, and oversize Roman pool with protected kiddie area. $3-5**

Coral Seas Motel, On the Ocean at Coral Street, Beach Haven, New Jersey. c. 1980. $2-3

Sierra Apartments, On the Beach at Amber Street, Beach Haven, N.J. c. 1961. Advertised on the reverse of the cards as "Modern Florida Type Apartments." The owners and operators were the Wittman, Wolfinger and Walders families. $2-5

Beach Haven Inlet Trailer Camp, Beach Haven, N.J. c. 1935. If you aren't a hotel kind of person, there was always one other option available – camping! Located on Harding Avenue, the Long Beach Island Trailer Park still operates today. $50-60

The Cottages
of Beach Haven

With the revision in 1876 of the map of Beach Haven by the Tuckerton and Long Beach Building & Land Improvement Association, the area of town that is today considered its Victorian heart was formally created. Stretching from just south of Marine Street to just north of Fifth Street, and from Atlantic Avenue to Bay Avenue, this area would ultimately encompass everything from large seaside cottages to small single-family homes, churches, hotels, and businesses.

The original center of town was located on Second Street where the Pharo and Smith cottages were built in 1874. Pharo, a "member of a Quaker family with American lineage dating to 1678," had these two homes constructed in a very simple style. It is easy to see, looking at them today, that they had much the look of a Quaker-style farmhouse. They are large enough to accommodate big families, with deep, shady porches to shelter the home's first floor from the blazing heat of the summer sun. Devoid of most of the architectural ornamentation that one generally associates with homes of this period, they were built solidly and practically.

Shortly after their construction, a very simple Quaker meeting house was erected just west of the Pharo cottage. This served the spiritual needs of a great many of the other early cottage builders who also happened to be of the Quaker faith. The homes that these people built were also large, like Pharo's, and fairly simple in design. They were by no means grandiose, yet there was an understated elegance about each of them. These homes were different from those that would be constructed a short while later in the newly laid out areas of town.

Pharo's Philadelphia business acquaintances set themselves up with quarters in the Parry House Hotel rather than in private cottages. With the loss of the Parry House by fire, the Philadelphia crowd moved their home base to the Hotel Baldwin for a number of summer seasons. At some point, however, they too decided to purchase lots and build summer homes of their own.

Coral Street, located midway between the Engleside and Baldwin Hotels, became the street that they chose and upon which they built their own castles in the sand. Philadelphia architect John Allston Wilson, of the firm of Wilson Brothers & Company, Architects, would design a great many of these homes. Both he, and later his descendents, would spend summers in one of his firm's own designs on Coral Street.

Some families decamped to Beach Haven for the entire summer season. Others, with vacation homes in other parts of the country, would spend only a portion of the summer at the beach. A great many of these homes were then rented out to other families when their owners were not in residence, much as they still are today.

As time passed, and these large homes began to fall out of favor, some were converted to guest houses and later to B&Bs. A fair number of these cottages remained in the hands of the families that built them, passed lovingly from generation to generation. It is only in recent years, as upkeep became onerous and family fortunes often diminished, that the final few have painfully been passed on to new owners. Louella Cottage, the Pharo family residence, is one of the very few that still remains in its original family's hands.

It is interesting to note that the homes in the main part of Beach Haven that were built along the length of Atlantic Avenue, facing the beach, were, for a great many years considered oceanfront homes. Starting in 1883, the land improvement company decided to offer the property owners on the west side of Atlantic Avenue the opportunity to purchase all of the property that existed across the street from each of them, excluding the fictional Seaside Avenue, and extending beyond that right out into the ocean. Most of the owners quickly exercised this option and the remainder followed suit within a short period of time. Only a few of these properties, located at the end of Second Street, remained on the books as unsold.

It has been said that a type of Gentleman's Agreement existed regarding the non-development of these properties. Except for the Engleside and Baldwin bath houses, and the boardwalks, this land remained fallow, with only a sandy stretch of dune grass and plank walks to the beach. Looking at images of it today, it seems almost unbelievable that all of this valuable property could have been allowed to just sit idle. It appears, though, that sometime after 1910 the aforementioned properties at the end of Second Street were sold off. Homes were then built on these lots, marking the first time that development had been allowed to cross Atlantic Avenue.

With the agreement seemingly no longer in effect and the current owners free to liquidate this property, the sales of these parcels began. Some of the first that would get sold were the lots lining the new boardwalk. Over time all of these lots were sold off by their owners, filling this block between Atlantic Avenue and the beach with a conglomeration of modern construction.

Today the historic core of Beach Haven remains relatively intact and remarkably untouched. Sadly, her grand hotels are both gone. A number of her historic cottages have been lost to fires, storms, or worse—overzealous development. However, in 2004, recognizing the importance of protecting what remains, the borough created a historic district in the heart of Victorian Beach Haven so that future generations of residents and visitors alike can continue to see what has always made her so special. These survivors of another age are finally safe.

To take an evening walk through the streets of this historic district is to feel a sense of what our ancestors felt as they walked her quiet gas-lit streets. With every footstep there is a palpable sense of history. It is easy to feel the reverberations of an earlier time as families relax on wide wooden porches and the sound of their friendly conversation floats on the air. Behind old screen doors, mothers trundle their sunburned children off to bed, while in the distance the ocean continues its incessant beating upon the shore. And somewhere in the night an old piano plays a tune of long ago.

Birds-Eye View of Beach Haven, N.J. c. 1925. This view, taken from the top of the town's water tower, looks directly up South Street towards the Engleside Hotel and out over the Victorian heart of Beach Haven. South Street would eventually be renamed Engleside Avenue. $40-60

North East Bird's Eye View, Beach Haven, N.J. c. 1920. This image, again taken from the Beach Haven water tower, looks out over the town north from Centre Street. The large building at the corner of Centre Street and Bay Avenue is the Beach Haven House Hotel. Just to the right of the center of this photo, east from the corner of Beach Avenue and Second Street, are the first two homes that Archelaus Pharo built in Beach Haven in 1874. This is considered the original 1874 section of town. $45-55

North East Bird's Eye View, Beach Haven, N. J.

View Looking North, Beach Haven, N. J.

View Looking North, Beach Haven, N.J. c. 1935. Taken from the roof of the Engleside Hotel, this view again looks out over the original settlement of Beach Haven. The block of houses, one block north, is where the Parry House stood until it burned in 1881. $8-12

ng North.   Beach Haven, N. J.

Atlantic Avenue Looking North, Beach Haven, N.J. c. 1925. Taken from the tower of the Engleside Hotel, this view looks north up Atlantic Avenue. The homes on the west side of Atlantic Avenue were oceanfront homes until the agreement about building east of Atlantic Avenue was broken with the construction of the home that is visible one block further north on Atlantic Avenue's east side. The home in the forefront, at the corner of Engleside and Atlantic Avenues, burned to the ground in the early 1980s while undergoing restoration. Today, the southern half of the Breaker's Condominiums sits on this site. $80-100

Breakers Cottage

100 CENTER ST.   BEACH HAVEN, N. J.

| Ocean Front Rooms |

PHONE 3-3481   MRS. A. L. WILLIAMS

Business Card, Breakers Cottage, Beach Haven, N.J. c. 1930. The Breakers Cottage, as it was then known, after serving as a private residence, was converted into a guest cottage where rooms were rented out on a daily and weekly basis by its owner, Mrs. A. L. Williams. $40-50

Beach Haven, N.J. "The Breakers Cottage". c. 1930. This real photo postcard shows one of Beach Haven's grandest Victorian era cottages. A smaller home once sat on this property at the corner of Centre Street and Atlantic Avenue; however, it was most likely moved to make room for this cottage around 1900. $175-350

Photograph, Interior View, Breakers Cottage, Beach Haven, N.J. c. 1905. These two images show what the interior of a typical seashore cottage looked like at the turn of the last century. They were often spacious and roomy, with fireplaces and many windows. The furnishings were an eclectic mix of wicker, and cast-offs from the family's town home, with a few family heirlooms thrown in for good measure. And no beach house was complete without a supply of fishing rods. $50

Photograph, Interior View, Breakers Cottage, Beach Haven, N.J. c. 1905. The Breakers cottage was renamed the Roman Villa in later years. It stood on this corner until the mid-1980s when it was purchased and demolished. Before demolition began, many residents of Beach Haven, following in the footsteps of their ancestors who salvaged what they could from wrecked ships, stripped the building of whatever re-usable parts and fixtures they could find for use in their own cottages. Today the northern half of the Breakers Condominiums sits on this site. $50

South St., Beach Haven, N. J.

South Street, Beach Haven, N.J. c. 1910. This view is taken from the center of South Street and Beach Avenue looking at the north side of South Street. The Holy Innocents Episcopal Church is on the corner and adjacent to it is a string of Victorian cottages. The large cottage to the right of center, with the steeply pitched roof, was one of the last of the great cottages to be built in Beach Haven. Designed in the Shingle Style, it is reminiscent of the type of cottages that were then being built at many of the wealthiest seashore resort towns. $135

North West View of Beach Haven, N.J. c. 1945. There is a real disparity in the messages that were written on these postcards sent from Beach Haven. People either loved it or hated it. Take for example these two messages. One writer pens, "Best wishes from Beach Haven. It's a lovely spot and we are enjoying every minute of our stay here." While another writes, "Dear Jennie, This is all I have seen of lovely Beach Haven. It is a sickening place if there ever was one. You might as well be in prison." $6-10

Street scene at Beach Haven, N. J.   McClure Pub.

Street Scene at Beach Haven, N.J. c. 1906. This view shows South Street looking west beyond Beach Avenue. Hopper's Store is on the left. It was a popular Mom & Pop type store that sold ice cream, candy, toys, and novelties. The Victorian homes west of Hopper's were more modest in size and were generally homes of full-time residents of Beach Haven. Many of these homes still exist. $100

Birds-Eye View   Beach Haven, N. J.

Birds-Eye View Beach Haven, N.J. c. 1925. This is another view from the water tower, this time looking southeast towards the Baldwin Hotel. This area of town would be the section that was laid out with the new map of 1876. Directly in the center is Coral Street, where the men from the Baldwin Locomotive Works built their cottages. $40-60

SALT AIR COTTAGE
Six Bedrooms, One Bath

These cottages have hot and cold water, gas for lighting purposes, and are fully furnished, including kitchen utensils, glass, china and silver.

For further information, apply to

E. L. WILSON
BEACH HAVEN, NEW JERSEY
PHONE 30

OR

WALTER W. PHARO
HAVERFORD, PA.
PHONE, ARDMORE 703

FURNISHED COTTAGES

BEACH HAVEN, NEW JERSEY
THE ISLAND RESORT SIX MILES AT SEA

PORTIA COTTAGE
Nine Bedrooms, Two Baths

Brochure, Furnished Cottages to Rent, Beach Haven, N.J. c. 1910. The family of architect John Allston Wilson was united with the family of Archelaus Pharo when Pharo's son Walter married Wilson's daughter Elizabeth. Each of the members of these two families owned a cottage in Beach Haven. As time passed, and family homes passed into these younger generation's hands, they were left with excess cottages. Instead of selling these extra homes, they rented them out. This brochure shows the homes that Emily Lloyd Wilson, and her sister Elizabeth Pharo, owned and had available to the public for rental. $50-60

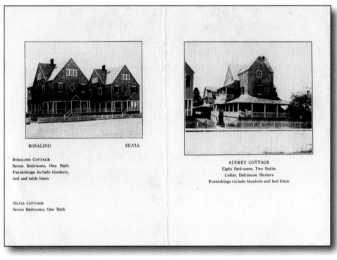

ROSALIND   SILVIA

ROSALIND COTTAGE
Seven Bedrooms, One Bath
Furnishings include blankets,
bed and table linen

AUDREY COTTAGE
Eight Bedrooms, Two Baths
Cellar, Baltimore Heaters
Furnishings include blankets and bed linen

SILVIA COTTAGE
Seven Bedrooms, One Bath

S. E. Bird's Eye View, Beach Haven, N. J.

S.E. Bird's Eye View, Beach Haven, N.J. c. 1920. Looking even further to the southeast, this postcard image encompasses what was then known as South Beach Haven. By 1920, a large number of smaller bungalow-style homes were being built in this growing section of town. $45-55

Brochure, Furnished Cottages to Rent, Beach Haven, N.J. c. 1910. Portia Cottage, also known today as Twin Chimneys, and designed by Wilson Brothers & Company, was originally owned by Dr. Edward Williams. When Williams decided he wanted a bigger, oceanfront home, he sold Portia Cottage to John Allston Wilson, the man who had designed it. Located on Coral Street, the property stretched all the way straight through the block to Amber Street. In later years, Wilson would build three homes for his daughters on the rear of the property. Known collectively as the Shakespeare Cottages, individually the cottages were named Rosalind, Silvia, and Audrey. Today all three are bed & breakfasts. Salt Air Cottage is located on Third Street and is today a privately owned cottage.

The Schealer House, 122 Amber Street, Beach Haven, N.J. c. 1949. By the 1940s, Silvia Cottage had become a guesthouse known as the Schealer House. Today it is part of the Victoria Guest House complex. $30-45

SOUTH EAST VIEW - BEACH HAVEN, N. J.

South East View, Beach Haven, N.J. c. 1928. This view, taken from the roof of the Engleside Hotel, looks down upon the cottages of Amber Street and towards the Baldwin Hotel. The cottage at the extreme right is the Shakespeare Cottage named Rosalind. Today it is the charming Amber Street Inn. $60-75

View from The Engleside.   Beach Haven, N. J.

View from The Engleside, Beach Haven, N.J. c. 1925. The cottage that is central to this image, once a private family cottage, is today known as the Windward Manor Inn. $20-30

Street Scene

Street Scene, Beach Haven, N.J. c. 1908. This view shows the north side of Coral Street, looking east, between Beach and Atlantic Avenues. This is without a doubt the most architecturally and historically significant block in all of Beach Haven. It was on this block that many of the principals of the Baldwin Locomotive Works built their cottages. Visible behind the tree is Florence Cottage, which belonged to Charles Parry's daughter. To the east is Portia Cottage, with its distinctive twin chimneys. At the end of the block is the Burnham Cottage, built for one of the partner-owners of the Baldwin Locomotive Works. This cottage was destroyed during the 1944 hurricane. $105

Beach Ave., Beach Haven, N.J. c. 1908. **This view looks north on Beach Avenue from the intersection at Pearl Street. $30-40**

Birdseye View from Hotel Baldwin, Beach Haven, N.J. c. 1908. **This view looks northwest towards the bay. Off in the distance is the Acme Hotel on Dock Road. $115**

Maker's mark on reverse of Souvenir China. c. 1910. Made by Millar China in Germany, this piece was retailed at Haidee Nakamura's Japanese Novelty Shop on the Beach Haven boardwalk.

Souvenir China, Birdseye View from Hotel Baldwin, Beach Haven, N.J. c. 1910. Here is the same view as was shown on the previous postcard reproduced on a piece of Souvenir China. $500

Birdseye View from Hotel Baldwin, Beach Haven, N.J. c. 1910. The cottages in the forefront of this image are directly across Pearl Street from where the Hotel Baldwin once stood. Beyond them are the backs of the cottages on Coral Street and further yet, the Engleside Hotel. $50-70

View from Board Walk, Beach Haven, N.J. c. 1908. No image gives better understanding to the story of the undeveloped property across from the cottages on Atlantic Avenue than this image does. It was just a wide sandy block of land from Atlantic Avenue to the boardwalk. The front of the cottage that you see on the left of this image is the Burnham Cottage. Just north are the cottages that are today the Sierra Guest House and the Windward Inn. Stretching beyond the Engleside are the remainders of the oceanfront cottages of Atlantic Avenue. $50-70

Ocean Avenue, Beach Haven, N.J. c. 1925. This misidentified postcard is actually Atlantic Avenue in front of the cottage that is now the Windward Inn. $100

The Waves Guest House and The Marine Apartments, 506 S. Atlantic Ave. & Ocean St., Beach Haven, N.J. c. 1953. These two cottages, near-mirror images of one another, still stand just south of the old Hotel Baldwin site. The cottage on the left was built for Dr. Edward Williams after he sold Portia Cottage. Today it is being restored for use as a bed & breakfast. The cottage on the right was built for John Converse. Converse and Williams were both partner-owners of the Baldwin Locomotive Works. Converse, a collector of Japanese art, named the cottage "Takiteze" as a nod to the influence of the Orient on his life and collecting. In reality, it was a play on the words, "take it easy." This cottage has been used as a guesthouse for a great many years. $100-125

Residence of Charles W. Beck, Beach Haven, N.J. c. 1920. This real photo postcard shows the property known in Beach Haven as the Beck Farm. Located on Liberty Avenue near the bay, the house was originally built for Thomas Sherborne. Beck, the owner of the Beck Engraving Company in Philadelphia, purchased the home and made extensive renovations and improvements to it, turning it into a real showplace. Today this home, located on a huge plot of land that has had developers salivating for years, remains safely in private hands. It is a true landmark of Beach Haven, which needs to be protected at all costs. The owner of this card penned on the reverse that the car shown in the driveway was called "the Pickle". $175-200

Private Residence, Beach Haven, N.J. c. 1940. Since it was built around 1920, this cottage has been known as the Lord Cottage after the family that built it. Located at the corner of Chatsworth and Atlantic Avenues, it was one of a series of large oceanfront homes built in the South Beach Haven development. It still stands today and it remains a private residence. $15-20

Beach Front Homes, Long Beach Island, N.J. c. 1945. With Beach Haven's Victorian cottage building days behind her, mid-century homeowners began building much more modest and affordable Cape Cod-style cottages. Plenty of these small houses remain throughout the community today. Unfortunately, the tide has now turned, and many of these homes are being demolished to make way for modern mega-monstrosities. Will we ever live long enough to see any of them considered classics of Jersey Shore architecture? It's doubtful. $3-7

Doing Business in Beach Haven

From her earliest days, Beach Haven's business district was located on Beach Avenue. This was the street that ran directly behind both the Engleside and Baldwin Hotels, serving as the community's main thoroughfare. Today it still retains a certain amount of this character, with the Surflight Theater and the Showplace Ice Cream Parlor anchoring one of its main blocks. If you look closely you can still see vestiges of other businesses in some of the old buildings that line it. Originally commercial structures that faced Beach Avenue, these buildings have all been converted to private residences.

Unlike Beach Avenue, Bay Avenue, one block to west, was laid out as a short strip of a street that connected a few blocks on the west side of Beach Haven, running no further north than Fourth Street. Except for the Beach Haven House, which had been built at the corner of Centre Street and Bay Avenue, and a few small homes and barns, there was very little else that existed there.

That all changed with the arrival of the automobile to Long Beach Island. The creation of Long Beach Boulevard as a thoroughfare to connect the entire island by automobile displaced Beach Avenue as Beach Haven's commercial center when it followed the path of Bay Avenue. Bay Avenue and Long Beach Boulevard remain the island's Main Street, and commercial heart, to this day.

Billhead, J.B. Cox & Son, Staple and Fancy Groceries, Dry Goods, Notions. c. 1898. Cox's Store was located on the corner of Beach Avenue and South Street in Beach Haven. $8-12

Beach and Centre Streets, Beach Haven, N.J. c. 1927. This postcard shows Beach Avenue looking south. Stores flank both sides of Beach Avenue. Peterson's store is on the left. On the right is Walsh's department store, the store that produced this fabulous set of postcards of Beach Haven. Today this is the home of the Show Place Ice Cream Parlor. $50-75

COX'S STORE & POST OFFICE, BEACH HAVEN, N.J.

July 11, 1911.

Cox's Store & Post Office, Beach Haven, N.J. c. 1911. This view of Cox's Store looks North on Beach Avenue from the corner of South Street. The small one-story building directly behind Cox's was the Beach Haven Post Office, and the building behind that is the rear of Hall's Store, which later became Walsh's department store. The message on this card is priceless. The sender writes, "Cox's Store where you can get everything – except the thing you want. Lots of the stores are just open in Summer." $190

CENTRAL PROVISION STORE - BEACH HAVEN, N. J.

Central Provision Store, Beach Haven, N.J. c. 1928. In later years, Cox's would be expanded and become the Central Provision Store. Today the Surflight Theater is built on this same site. $55-65

Photograph, Member of the Beach Haven Beach Patrol and Mailman, South Street and Beach Avenue. c. 1930. This photo is taken looking west on South Street. The Central Provision Store is over the shoulders of these two fellows. $12-16

Photograph, Ice Delivery Truck, South Street, Beach Haven, N.J. c. 1930. This photograph is taken in front of the Central Garage on South Street between Beach and Bay Avenues. Notice the giant pair of ice tongs in the hands of the deliveryman. The Central Garage was later the home of the Surflight Theater. $20-30

Photograph, Lifeguards on South Street. c. 1930. This photograph of members of the Beach Haven Beach Patrol is taken in the middle of South Street, looking east towards the beach. The Central Provision Store is on the left and the Steeple of Holy Innocents Church is behind them. $15-20

Surflight Summer Theater, Beach Haven, N.J. c. 1960. Founded in 1950 by Joseph P. Hayes, the Surflight Theater originally performed its productions in a tent in Beach Haven Crest. In 1954, they would move to this building as a permanent home. $10-15

Surflight Summer Theater, Beach Haven, N.J. c. 1965. Joe Hayes died in 1976, but his theater has lived on. Today the original theater building is used as the theater's scenery shop, while productions have moved into a modern air-conditioned structure next door, built on the site of Cox's Store. $10-15

A. J. Durand, Pharmacy, Beach Haven, N. J.

A. J. Durand Pharmacy, Beach Haven, N.J. c. 1910. The Durand Pharmacy was located on the corner of Beach Avenue and Pearl Street in the lower level of the Hotel Baldwin Annex. From the appearance of this photo, it looks as though there was a soda fountain that you could walk up to from the street. We have Mr. Durand to thank for a beautiful series of postcards of Beach Haven. $180

Lamb's Seafood Restaurant, Bay and Centre Sts., Beach Haven, N.J. Richard Lamb, Prop. c. 1935. This building was built in two phases. The part on the left was built on the corner of the property where Lamb's Beach Haven House Hotel sat. Wanting to expand the restaurant business, the old hotel was moved to the back of the property and the right side of the building was built. Today this building is Buckalew's Restaurant and Bar. $15-20

Bay Avenue, Beach Haven, N.J. c. 1930. With the opening of Long Beach Boulevard, Bay Avenue became the island's Main Street. This view looking at the west side of Bay Avenue in Beach Haven was taken just about in the middle of the block between Engleside Avenue and Centre Street, looking north. The building in the center of the photo is the Colonial Theater, and just to its left, across Centre Street, was Britz's Restaurant and Bar. The building on the left side of the image was the home of the Frankfurt Pharmacy. They published and sold a great many postcards of Beach Haven, including this one. $55-60

Bay Avenue, Beach Haven, N.J. c. 1925. This is a similar view of Bay Avenue, but looking straight up the boulevard, and showing both sides of the street. The building on the right is where Uncle Will's Pancake House is now located, and next to that is Paxson's Pharmacy, which is now known as Kapler's. Just beyond that is the old Beach Haven House Hotel. $45-50

Bay Avenue, Beach Haven, N.J. c. 1938. A later view taken from the intersection of Engleside Avenue and Bay Avenue. The corner lot remains empty, but smaller commercial structures have been built adjacent to the Uncle Will's building. $6-10

Bay Avenue, Beach Haven, N.J.

Bay Avenue, Beach Haven, N.J. c. 1945. By the time this postcard was made, the Beach Haven House had been moved and Lamb's Restaurant had been built. On the corner of Engleside and Bay Avenues, the ACME Supermarket had been built. Today this is Murphy's Supermarket. $6-10

COLONIAL THEATRE   BEACH HAVEN, N. J.

Colonial Theater, Beach Haven, N.J. c. 1930. Built by Harry Colmer in 1922, the Colonial Theater at the corner of Centre Street and Bay Avenue would continue showing movies until the end of the summer season of 2003. Seeing a movie in this old building in the middle of summer could be a very suffocating experience! The building has since been rehabbed and is now the Beach Haven branch store of the Tuckerton Lumber Company. $100

Business Section, Looking South, Beach Haven, Long Beach, N.J. c. 1945. This is a view of Bay Avenue looking south from the middle of the block between Second and Third Streets. The law offices and home of lawyer Julius Robinson are today located on the corner of Second Street and Bay Avenue where the square house sits in this image. That structure was moved to the end of Second Street, near the dunes, and reused for housing. To the right of that building is Lamb's Restaurant, and back behind it is visible the old Beach Haven House Hotel. $10-15

BUSINESS SECTION, LOOKING SOUTH, BEACH HAVEN, LONG BEACH, N.J.

Village Pub & Restaurant, Center's Crossing and Bay Avenue, Beach Haven, N.J. c. 1970. In the 1970s, the building that for a great many years had served as Britz's Bar became the Village Pub & Restaurant. Today this building houses the Marlin Restaurant & Bar. $3-6

"INLET INN"
Wm. DeFreitas, Jr., Prop.
Beach Haven Inlet, N. J.

12016

"Inlet Inn" Wm. DeFreitas, Jr. Prop., Beach Haven Inlet, N.J. c. 1935. The Inlet Inn was located just south of downtown Beach Haven at the corner of Roosevelt and West Avenue. Popular with the crowds that flocked to the inlet for the fishing, the Inn was completely destroyed in the Hurricane of 1944. Original Photograph from which the postcard was made, $50.

Churches, Buildings, and Other Structures

In addition to her businesses and cottages, Beach Haven was, and still is, the home to a great number of other buildings and structures. Churches, schools, clubhouses, and piers were built at various times and for a variety of purposes, and almost all of these were documented on postcards.

M.E. Church at Beach Haven, N.J. c. 1906. This postcard mistakenly identifies this as the M.E. Church when in actuality it is the Holy Innocents Episcopal Church. This structure, located at the corner of Beach Avenue and Engleside Avenue in Beach Haven, owes its existence to the disastrous fire at the Parry House Hotel. Mrs. Charles Parry, who had been staying in the hotel at the time of the conflagration, was so grateful that there had been no loss of life that she gave this church to Beach Haven in thanksgiving. Designed by Wilson Brothers & Company, this fabulous structure was originally adorned in high Victorian fashion. Of special note was the highly decorated verge board in the south-facing gable of the church with its stylized, intertwined Alpha and Omega symbols. $45-60

Episcopal Church, Beach Haven, N.J. c.1926. The church building was given in memory of Clara Parry Hilger, a daughter of the Parrys who had recently died in childbirth. The name Holy Innocents was chosen to recognize all children who had predeceased their parents. In 1903, a storm blew the church from its foundations and felled the great tower. It was decided at that time to move the church eastward on its lot when it was reconstructed. $20-25

1240   Episcopal Church, Beach Haven, N. J.

Church of the Holy Innocents (Episcopal) Beach & Engleside Avenues, Beach Haven, New Jersey. c. 1965. At some point prior to 1925, most likely due to the severe maintenance issues encountered at the shore, it was decided to strip much of the detail from the exterior of the building and replace it with the classic seashore cedar shake shingle exterior that you see today. In 1938, a winter chapel was built just east of the main sanctuary so that the church, which until that point had only been used in summers, could be used all year round. $3-6

Holy Innocents Episcopal Church, Marine Street, Beach Haven, N.J. c. 1975. In 1974, the congregation purchased the site of the old Hotel Baldwin and on it constructed a new sanctuary. They moved a number of the historic items from the old church into the new structure; including the spectacular aesthetic movement stained glass window that had been over the altar. The old church building was then purchased by the Long Beach Island Historical Association. In their thirty-five-year existence, they have accumulated an odd collection of wedding gowns and household objects that they feel somehow tells a story about the history of Long Beach Island. $2-4

An Every Day Scene at Beach Haven N.J.   McClure Pub

An Every Day Scene at Beach Haven, N.J. c. 1905. This view, looking north on Beach Avenue, would have been taken standing next to Holy Innocents in the heart of what was then downtown Beach Haven. The building in the middle of the image, in the middle of the block on Beach Avenue between Centre Street and Second Street, is Kynett Methodist Church. This congregation was founded in 1888. They built this structure in 1891. $35-45

M.E. Church, Beach Haven, N.J.
c. 1908. The same storm in September
of 1903 that blew Holy Innocents from
its foundations also affected Kynett
by toppling its huge steeple. And just
as at Holy Innocents, in the process
of reconstructing the church after the
storm, the congregation decided to
move the structure south to the corner
of the block. The steeple, which had
long been a mariner's landmark, was
not rebuilt. $30-40

1256   The Methodist Church, Beach Haven, N. J.

*The Methodist Church,
Beach Haven, N.J.*
c. 1925. This building
would serve the
members of Kynett
Methodist until it was
destroyed by fire in
March of 1932. $30-40

*Kynette Methodist
Church, Beach Haven,
N.J.* c. 1935. After the fire
the congregation sprang
into action, building and
dedicating a new church
by Christmas of 1932.
Dedicated in August of
1933, Kynett continues
to serve the Methodist
congregation of Beach
Haven to this day. $3-5

Kynette Methodist Church, Beach Haven, N.J. c. 1970. $2-4

Catholic Church, Beach Haven, N.J. c. 1911. Catholic services have been held in Beach Haven since 1885. A small chapel was built in 1891, but by the end of the decade, with attendance increasing, it was felt that a more substantial sanctuary should be built. Church fathers called upon Philadelphia architect Edwin Forrest Durang, one of the city's best known designers of Catholic churches, to draw up plans for a new church in Beach Haven. This postcard shows the church that Durang designed. It was built on a lot at the corner of Fourth Street and Beach Avenue in 1899. $20-30

Catholic Church and Rectory, Beach Haven, N.J. c. 1908. In December of 1907, church fathers called upon Philadelphia architect Henry D. Dagit, the leading competitor of E. F. Durang in designing Catholic structures, to design a rectory for them at Beach Haven. This imposing structure, built at the corner of Third Street and Beach Avenue, would serve the church until the 1980s, when it was demolished to build a new church-owned residence on the site. $35-45

St. Thomas Catholic Church, Beach Haven, N.J. c. 1941. This church would serve the Catholics of Beach Haven until 1965, when a much larger church was built at the corner of Second Street and Atlantic Avenue. Today this structure, covered in aluminum siding that hides all of its beautiful detail, sits empty and is used for storage. $5-10

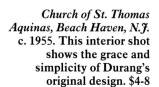

Church of St. Thomas Aquinas, Beach Haven, N.J. c. 1955. This interior shot shows the grace and simplicity of Durang's original design. $4-8

THE LIBRARY, Beach Haven, N. J.

The Library, Beach Haven, N.J. c. 1917. This building was the original Quaker Meeting House that had once stood at the corner of Second Street and Beach Avenue. In 1905, it was donated by the Pharo family to the community to be used as a public library. It was moved a half a block away, on Beach Avenue, to where the Kynett Church had stood prior to the storm of 1903. It would serve as the town's library until 1924, at which time it was donated to Kynett Methodist Church to serve as a parish house, a function that it still serves to this day. $120-150

106

Public Library, Beach Haven, N.J. c. 1929. **This handsome structure, designed by architect R. Brognard Okie, a relative of the Pharo family through marriage, was donated to Beach Haven by Elizabeth Wilson Pharo in 1924. Elizabeth, a daughter of architect John Allston Wilson, was married to Walter W. Pharo, son of Archelaus Pharo, founder of Beach Haven. She gave the library in memory of her late husband and his parents. It stands at the corner of Beach Avenue and Third Street. $25-35**

VIEW OF BEACH HAVEN, N. J., PUBLIC LIBRARY.

VIEW OF BEACH HAVEN, N. J., PUBLIC LIBRARY.

View of Beach Haven, N.J. Public Library. c. 1925. Okie was "one of the most adept practitioners of the Colonial Revival style" and he brought all of his skills to bear on the design that he came up with for the library. It is a masterwork of design that is worthy of much more recognition than it currently receives. Okie felt no detail was too small, and designed everything right down to the hinges and the light fixtures. Today this structure remains virtually untouched, and to be able to gaze upon its beauty is to be able to see it through the eyes of its creator. $5-10

View of Beach Haven, N.J., Public Library. c. 1925. The brick used in the floors of the library came from St. John's Church in Philadelphia. Okie had it salvaged for re-use in the library, as the church was being demolished to make way for the Benjamin Franklin Bridge approach. It is said that the brick had actually come to Philadelphia as ballast in ships prior to its having been used to construct the church. $5-10

VIEW OF BEACH HAVEN, N. J., PUBLIC LIBRARY.

View of Beach Haven, N.J., Public Library. c. 1925. On the second floor of the library, and through a small door, is a special museum collection that documents the history of Long Beach Island. That room is pictured on this postcard. The museum collection contains everything from artwork, to photographs, to old hotel registers. $5-10

PUBLIC SCHOOL · BEACH HAVEN, N. J.

Public School, Beach Haven, N.J. c. 1928. Built in 1912, this structure has continued to serve the educational needs of Beach Haven's children ever since. $25-30

Corinthian Yacht & Gun Club, Beach Haven, N.J. c. 1908. Founded in 1903 as the Beach Haven Gun Club, this organization changed its name to the Corinthian Yacht and Gun Club in 1907. The club's focus of activity was centered on sport shooting and, with the name change, also amateur sailing. Their clubhouse, located at the corner of Marine Street and Beach Avenue, was a homey place that was used primarily in the off-season when the Hotel Baldwin had closed. By 1911, the club came to the realization that they needed to discontinue operations. They were too far from the water to be a real yacht club, and with more houses being built, their area for sport shooting was getting dangerous. The clubhouse was sold and became a private residence. It was demolished in 1984. $25-35

CORINTHIAN YACHT & GUN CLUB, BEACH HAVEN, N. J.

1247   Electric Plant and Plants Water Works,
Beach Haven, N. J.

Electric Plant and Plants Water Works, Beach Haven, N.J. c. 1925. This water tower was actually the second one to be built in Beach Haven. It replaced an earlier timber water tower that had been built in 1895. This water tower would eventually be replaced by the current tower. $25-30

Fishing Pier, Waterfront, Beach Haven, N. J.

Fishing Pier, Waterfront, Beach Haven, N.J. c. 1942. This huge fishing pier was located at the ocean end of Berkeley Avenue in what was then called South Beach Haven. It was built in 1924, and all but a few pilings were swept away in the Hurricane of 1944. $5-7

Fishing Pier   Beach Haven, N. J.

Fishing Pier, Beach Haven, N.J. c. 1928. $50

The Fishing Pier, Beach Haven, N.J. c. 1937. The message on a postcard sent from Beach Haven in 1925 stated, "Well Harry, old Beach Haven is still here, very quiet though. The Pier is open for everyone to fish on. All they get at the Pier is Skates and Dog Sharks." $50

Dock Road

While walking the streets that encircle the end of Dock Road in the vicinity of The Ketch nightclub and The Boat House restaurant, few would have any idea of the role that this section of town once played in the development of Beach Haven. Today Dock Road is a paved street that angles its way from Bay Avenue all the way back to the bay. But when Archelaus Pharo decided on the location for his new seashore community it was primarily due to its proximity with Mud Hen Creek, a creek that once paralleled today's Dock Road.

Mud Hen Creek, a natural waterway through the marshes, provided convenient water access directly to the heart of Beach Haven. This made it easy to barge material and supplies right to the construction sites of the future hotels and cottages. Then a road was built across the marshes and adjacent to the creek. Further development would create a public wharf at the end of this road.

For a number of years, the only structure of any significance located at the end of Dock Road was Captain Tilton Fox's Hotel DeCrab. Eventually the Beach Haven Yacht Club was built at the very end of the wharf, and around 1900, the Acme Hotel was constructed between it and the Hotel DeCrab. After a number of years, the creek was completely filled in, and all that remains to remind us of it today is Dock Road and its angled path into the heart of Beach Haven.

Hotel De Crab and owner, Captain Tilton Fox. c. 1910. **Fox bought a decommissioned House of Refuge that had been originally located in Harvey Cedars. These were structures that were placed along the New Jersey coast to serve as shelter for victims of shipwrecks and also as a place to store the equipment needed for life saving purposes. Fox barged the old structure down to Beach Haven and placed it up on pilings over Mud Hen Creek, adjacent to what would become Dock Road. This is an extremely rare image to find, as nowhere on it does it mention Beach Haven. So most people who see it have no idea where it comes from. $150-175**

Hotel De Crab, Beach Haven, N. J.

Hotel De Crab, Beach Haven, N.J. c. 1908. Fox's Hotel De Crab catered to the party boat captains whose vessels lay anchored nearby in the bay. Captain Fox and his wife ran the hotel from 1872 until 1917 when they decided to sell it. Shellfish must have been popular at the hotel. Notice the huge mound of cast-off shells that lay at the base of the rear steps. This building, most likely the oldest structure in Beach Haven, survived until the mid-1980s, at which time it was demolished with very little fanfare or recognition of its historic value to the community. $150-175

Engleside Hotel Advertising Card, Winter Scene, Dock Road, Beach Haven, N.J. c. 1907. Unless you've spent a winter on Long Beach Island, you can't fully appreciate the teeth-chattering feeling that you get when you see this postcard of the frozen bay. Taken at the very end of Dock Road with the Acme Hotel on the left and Beach Haven off in the distance, this was a card sent out by the Engleside Hotel to remind people that summer was coming and that they hoped you would return again for a visit. $40-60

Hotel Acme, Beach Haven, Ocean County, New Jersey, An Ideal Summer Resort. John W. Cranmer, Proprietor. c. 1907. The Acme Hotel shown on this card opened for business in 1904. Prior to that date, the smaller building, attached to the rear of this structure, served as the hotel. This building survives today and is known as the Ketch. $80-90

Marshall's Restaurant, Beach Haven, N. J.

Marshall's Restaurant, Beach Haven, N.J. c. 1910. This structure was located just beyond the Hotel Acme, right next to the Beach Haven Yacht Club. Very little is known of its inception or ownership. In later years it would be called Parker's Restaurant and also the Public Dock Hotel. $120-140

Public Dock Hotel,
Beach Haven, N.J.
c. 1925. $120-140

1249   Public Dock Hotel, Beach Haven, N. J.

each Haven Yacht Club, Beach Haven, N. J.

Beach Haven Yacht Club, Beach Haven, N.J.
c. 1908. The Beach Haven Yacht Club was
founded by one of Beach Haven's summer
residents, Charles Gibbons, Jr., in the mid-1880s.
Unlike many of the yacht clubs we think of today,
the membership of this club was focused
primarily on the local fishing boat captains. $65

Boat Landing at Little Egg Harbor, Beach Haven,
N.J. c. 1910. The club was a beautiful two-story
building with wide porches. It was built out on
pilings over the marshes at the end of Dock
Road and served as the social center of the
yacht club. Here the boat captains gathered for
drinks and camaraderie in the club's bar. $10-15

Boat Landing at Little Egg Harbor, Beach Haven N. J.

52-4

Beach Haven Yacht Club.   Beach Haven, N. J.

Beach Haven Yacht Club, Beach
Haven, N.J. c. 1915. $15-20

Wharf and Yacht Club, Beach Haven, N.J. c. 1906. This is a good image in that it shows the viewer where exactly these buildings all were in relation to one another. In the center is the Beach Haven Yacht Club on the site where Morrison's Restaurant stood for many years. To the right of center is the Acme Hotel, today known as The Ketch, and behind it is the Hotel De Crab. All the way on the right, where water is shown, is where the Boat House restaurant is located today. $35-45

The Wharf and Club House, Beach Haven, N.J. c. 1905. $10-12

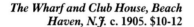

Club House at Beach Haven, N.J. c. 1906. Most of the boats that sailed from the Beach Haven Yacht Club were the majestic catboats. When in full sail, they made for a breathtaking sight. $15-20

The Fleet, Beach Haven, N.J. c. 1906. The long, curving wharf of the Beach Haven Yacht Club was a landmark for years. Most of the fishing parties chartered through the captains of the Beach Haven Yacht Club, left from this wharf. $5-10

Dock Scene, Beach Haven, N.J. c. 1914. Sent to Reading, Pa., in August of 1914, the sender writes, "Am having a fine time – plenty of water to swim in – also one can drown all their sorrows there in." signed, Miss F. Levan. $8-10

The Dock, Beach Haven, N.J. c. 1905. $8-12

The Dock, Beach Haven, N.J. c. 1910. The other style of boat that often appears in yacht club photographs and postcards is the Barnegat Bay Sneakbox, pictured so prominently in this image. $12-14

Beach Haven Yacht Club Wharf, Beach Haven, N.J.

Beach Haven Yacht Club Wharf, Beach Haven, N.J. dated July 20, 1910. "Landed here this morning. Am feeling well again got a lot of blue fish yesterday." $10-12

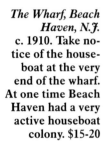

The Wharf   Beach Haven, N. J.

The Wharf, Beach Haven, N.J. c. 1910. Take notice of the houseboat at the very end of the wharf. At one time Beach Haven had a very active houseboat colony. $15-20

Yacht Club Dock, Beach Haven, N.J. c. 1925. $25-30

1239   Yacht Club Dock, Beach Haven, N. J.

YACHT CLUB DOCK, BEACH HAVEN, N. J.

Fishing Dock, Beach Haven, N. J.

Fishing Dock, Beach Haven, N.J. c. 1925. Mud Hen Creek was filled in around the same time that the automobile arrived for good on the island. The wharf continued to expand to accommodate the motorists that began pouring onto the island. $30-40

Yacht Club Dock, Beach Haven, N.J. c. 1930. With the advent of the gasoline engine, sail power was no longer required to propel the fleet. Many of the majestic catboats were shorn of their sails and their masts were removed when they were converted over to engine power. The grace and beauty of these boats was lost in the process. $8-12

YACHT CLUBS AND PUBLIC DOCK, BEACH HAVEN, N. J.

Yacht Clubs and Public Dock, Beach Haven, N.J. c. 1932. $6-10

Morrison's Restaurant & Marina. c. 1958. In 1930, the Beach Haven Yacht Club was forced to either purchase the land upon which it was sitting or vacate the premises. It seems that for years they had been on somebody else's land! The club decided to pick up their building and move it, rather than give in and buy the land it sat on. Instead, they purchased a bay front lot a few blocks further south, and re-established themselves there. In 1946, Morrison's Fishery, which would later become Morrison's Restaurant, began to do business on the old yacht club site. $5-10

Morrison's Seafood Restaurant. c. 1965. Morrison's Restaurant was a typical seashore-style restaurant and no visit to Beach Haven was ever complete without at least one meal at Morrison's. Sadly, after almost sixty years in business, Morrison's burned to the ground in September of 2005. $5-10

Yacht Club, Beach Haven, N.J. c. 1935. This image shows the club at its new location on West Avenue between Centre Street and Engleside Avenue. $5-10

Beach Haven Yacht Club and Dock, Beach Haven, N.J. c. 1938. $20-25

Boats at Yacht Club, Beach Haven, N.J. c. 1934. $10-15

Beach Haven Yacht Club Docks, Beach Haven, N.J. c. 1935. **Original Dexter Press photograph from which the postcard would have been produced, $25.**

Beach Haven Yacht Club, Beach Haven, N.J. c. 1962.
The Beach Haven Yacht Club flourished at its new location. A succession of club managers developed it into one of the best private dining clubs on the island. $5-8

Beach Haven Yacht Club, Beach Haven, N.J. c. 1961. The club building would survive until 1985, when club members decided to sell the property. The contents were auctioned off and the building was demolished. Today there are condominiums where the Beach Haven Yacht Club used to be. $3-5

Priestley's Marina, Beach Haven, N.J. c. 1960. $4-8

Aerial View of Yacht Club and Shoreline, Beach Haven, N.J. c. 1962. This image is a good one because it shows the juxtaposition of old and new. Within the core of the club building the steeply hipped roofline of the old Beach Haven Yacht Club structure is still visible. $6-10

Little Egg Harbor Yacht Club

The creation of the Little Egg Harbor Yacht Club on June 12, 1912, is credited to Elmer Weidner. The story has it that the club began when Mr. Weidner was busy building a dock on the bay for his sneakbox named the *Tonik*. He was assisted in this project by a friend named Tom Annadown. Eventually others would join in their dock-building venture and from this enterprise would grow the LEHYC.

The founding of the LEHYC has as much to do with this story of Mr. Weidner and his dock as it has to do with the dissolution of Beach Haven's old Corinthian Yacht & Gun Club. This club had consisted of primarily summer dwellers of the town, unlike the Beach Haven Yacht Club, which centered on the local fishing boat captains. The Corinthian had folded in 1911, leaving the summer crowd with no place to call home. So the small informal group of individuals that had gathered to build Mr. Weidner's dock decided that a new club was needed.

Charles Beck, owner of the Beck Engraving Company in Philadelphia, who resided at the Beck Farm on Liberty Avenue in Beach Haven, was elected as the club's first Commodore. By 1916 the group, which was made up primarily of the old Corinthian members, built a spectacular clubhouse on the bay. It is a beautiful example of shingle-style construction with very clean lines and classical embellishments. It still stands today, very much unchanged from its original appearance; a true seashore classic if ever there was one.

LITTLE EGG HARBOR YACHT CLUB, BEACH HAVEN, N. J.

Little Egg Harbor Yacht Club, Beach Haven, N.J. c. 1935. $15-25

Little Egg Harbor Yacht Club, Beach Haven, N. J.

Little Egg Harbor Yacht Club, Beach Haven, N.J. c. 1927. $30-50

Little Egg Harbor Yacht Club, Beach Haven, N.J. c. 1936. $5-10

Little Egg Harbor Yacht Club, Beach Haven, N.J. c. 1938. $20-30

Little Egg Harbor Yacht Club, Beach Haven, N.J. c. 1941. $5-8

Egg Harbor Yacht Club   Beach Haven, N. J.

Little Egg Harbor Yacht Club, Beach Haven, N.J. c. 1935. $30-35

View from the Front of the Little Egg Yacht Club, Beach Haven, N. J.

View from the Front of the Little Egg Yacht Club, Beach Haven, N.J. c. 1940. $6-8

Shoreline From Little Egg Harbor Yacht Club, Beach Haven, N.J. c. 1963. $3-5

The *Lucy Evelyn*

Built in Harrington, Maine, in 1917, and named for the builder's two daughters, the schooner *Lucy Evelyn* arrived in Beach Haven in the summer of 1948 and remained one of Long Beach Island's premier tourist attractions for almost a quarter of a century. The story of the *Lucy Evelyn's* sojourn in Beach Haven began with the destruction wrought upon the island by the horrendous Hurricane of 1944. Nat & Betty Ewer, owners of the Sea Chest store on the boardwalk in Beach Haven, lost their entire store and inventory to the storm-tossed waves. Afterwards they re-opened with a shop in the Baldwin Hotel.

A few years later, while vacationing in New England, the Ewers heard about a ship that was going to be auctioned off. Deciding that this might make a perfect replacement for their Sea Chest, they bid on the ship and succeeded in winning the auction. The *Lucy Evelyn* was towed to Beach Haven. There she sat in the bay for most of the summer of 1948, awaiting the high tides that would be needed to get her over the shoals and onto dry land where the Ewers planned to beach the enormous ship and convert her into their new store.

On a stormy and harrowing night in October of that year, with the tides rising fast, the ship was sailed over the shoals and into the island's mud banks at the bay end of Ninth Street. After dredging a huge basin in front of the ship, she was sailed into it on another stormy night of rising tides the following month. Crews immediately went to work replacing the water that surrounded her with sand. Her seagoing travels had finally ended.

The schooner *Lucy Evelyn* was scrubbed and polished and converted into a retail establishment, opening the following year for her first summer season on Long Beach Island. Business was very good, and eventually buildings were built surrounding her that housed additional retail ventures. The success of this entire complex, originally on the outer fringe of Beach Haven, would help to extend northwards the business center of the town, virtually doubling the length of her business district on Bay Avenue.

Sadly, on a frigid early February night in 1972, the *Lucy Evelyn* caught fire and burned. At the end of the three-day-long fire, nothing of the fantastic old ship was left but a smoldering pile of ruins. In the end, a new complex of shops known as Schooner's Wharf was built to replace her. It even included a landlocked ship as part of the design. But to those who knew and loved the *Lucy Evelyn*, it was nice but just not the same. Fortunately for us, through the magic of picture postcards, entire generations of youngsters and oldsters alike can still experience the charms of the *Lucy Evelyn* and Nat and Betty Ewer's Sea Chest.

The Schooner "Lucy Evelyn", 140' Long, 32" Beam, 10" Draft, Built 1917 in Harrington, Maine, Beached and Preserved 1949, Beach Haven, N.J. c. 1950. $8-12

The Schooner "Lucy Evelyn", Beach Haven, N. J.

The Schooner "Lucy Evelyn", Beach Haven, N.J. The Home of THE SEA CHEST Gift and Sport Shops. c. 1952. $6-8

Seaman's Shack and Schooner Lucy Evelyn Beach Haven, N. J.

The Schooner Lucy Evelyn, Beach Haven, N.J. c. 1958. Take note as to how much open space still existed at the time this photograph was taken. None of the Bay Village complex even existed at this point in time. $5-7

Seaman's Shack and Schooner Lucy Evelyn, Beach Haven, N.J. c. 1960. $4-6

Beach Haven, N.J. c. 1965. $5-7

Schooner Lucy Evelyn, Beach Haven, New Jersey. c. 1969. $4-6

The Schooner Lucy Evelyn at Sunset, Long Beach Island, N.J. c. 1968. $4-6

Seaman's Shack. One of Long Beach Island's Oldest Houses. c. 1965. This structure was reported to have come from a property in the vicinity of the Spray Beach Hotel. It was actually an old gunning shack, not a house. It still sits at the rear of the Schooner's Wharf complex of shops. $2-4

Schooner's Christmas Cargo, Beach Haven, New Jersey. c. 1965. $3-6

"Wharf Rats", Jolly Pound Boat, Schooner "Lucy Evelyn", Beach Haven, New Jersey. c. 1965. This unlikely amphitheater, created from a pound fishing boat turned on its side, was a venue for then-popular folk music. Groups like the Wharf Rats played there in the 1960s. $25-30

Famous Country Kettle Fudge Shop, Schooner's Wharf, Beach Haven, N.J. c. 1965. This is the original location of the fudge shop that vacationers to Long Beach Island enjoy visiting. It would later move across the street as one of the anchor businesses in the Bay Village complex of shops. $6-10

Shelter Harbor Marina, 317 11th Street, Beach Haven, N.J. c. 1965. Shelter Harbor Marina is located directly adjacent to the *Lucy Evelyn* in this photograph. Much of this site has since been developed into condominiums and retail shopping in addition to the marina. $7-10

Chapter 3
Go Fish!

Sport fishing has been drawing visitors to Long Beach Island since the earliest days. I guess you could say that the Native Americans who visited her shores were really the first of her sport fishermen! We know that many of the men who traveled to Bond's Long Beach House came for just this reason. In later years, visitors to the island sent postcard after postcard upon which they penned the details of their day's fishing expedition. And so it continues to this day. Whether it is deep-sea fishing, fishing in the bay, or surf fishing, Long Beach Island continues to be a haven for the sport fisherman.

Beach Haven House, Beach Haven, N.J. **c. 1920. The Beach Haven House catered to the gunning and fishing crowd, as evidenced by the images on this postcard. $35-40**

Blue Marlin, Long Beach Island, N.J. c. 1938. $4-6

Going Fishing at Beach Haven. **c. 1938. "My Dear Boy, Have not forgotten you, but I am leading a strenuous life. Out fishing twice, total catch to date 117 fish and one three foot shark." $10-15**

Channel bass with rod and reel, Surf at Beach Haven, N.J. **c. 1919. It seems the idea of surf fishing had never been thought of on Long Beach Island before 1907. In that year, Mr. & Mrs. Charles E. Gerhard of Beach Haven shocked their fellow townspeople by wading into the water while attired in bathing suits, and began casting. After a hard thirty-minute fight, Mrs. Gerhard hauled in a twenty-pound channel bass, or drum fish as the species is also known. People were amazed at the catch and the idea of surf fishing quickly caught on. The sender of this card, J.F. Ives, claims that this is his picture on the front of the card. Whether that is the truth, or just a bit of leg pulling, isn't clear. This image was taken next to the porte-cochere of the Engleside Hotel on Engleside Avenue. $65**

Surf Fishing Harvey Cedars, N. J.
"Between the Atlantic Ocean and Barnegat Bay"

Surf Fishing, Harvey Cedars, N.J. c. 1930. "Your friend Mr. Clark caught 18 weak fish Monday night; last night caught one and his pole broke, but it is being mended today and will be ready tomorrow." $30-40

Unloading Catch of Tuna Fish. Beach Haven. N. J.

Unloading Catch of Tuna Fish, Beach Haven, N.J. c. 1940. $6-9

Trophies of the Sea, Beach Haven, N.J. c. 1946. "My Dear Young Friend, We are having a fine time we caught 80 fish today. From Uncle John." $5-7

The Morning's Catch
Beach Haven, N. J.

The Morning's Catch, Beach Haven, N.J. c. 1935. Original photograph for postcard, $18-22.

Tuna Fishing Boats, Long Beach Island, N.J. c. 1958. $3-5

Cruiser Sea Spray, Beach Haven Yacht Club, Beach Haven, N.J. Capt. Fred Nichterlein. c. 1946. $15-20

Fishing Boats, Long Beach Island. c. 1956. $4-8

Chapter 4
On Barnegat Bay
& Little Egg Harbor

Ask anybody to describe the communities on Long Beach Island and eventually, somewhere in the discussion, reference will be made to the "ocean side" and the "bay side" of whatever part of the island they happen to be talking about. It's the same thing with the people on Long Beach Island. There are ocean people and then there are bay people. Long Beach Boulevard is the imaginary demarcation line that divides towns and people into the two camps.

Ocean people, quite simply, live for the beach, while bay people embrace everything about what makes the bay so special. For most there are a variety of things that attract them to the bay. For many it is the sailing and for others the sunsets. The wildlife, the bay beaches, and the sedge islands all hold a special attraction for those who consider themselves bay people.

But it is probably sailing, and a love of boats, that attracts the majority of these people to the bay. Many have homes with private docks or boat slips at the yacht clubs and marinas of the island. Sailing is a tradition that is passed from generation to generation on LBI where homes are often adorned with yacht club burgees and the mantelpiece is lined with trophy cups from yacht races of long ago.

The tradition of sailing on Barnegat Bay and Little Egg Harbor is a long and storied one. And it is one that is well documented in photographs and vintage postcards, a selection of which has been chosen here.

Sailing down Barnegat Bay. **c. 1909. This is probably one of the most beautiful images ever produced of ships on the bay. $40**

Out on Barnegat Bay, N.J. c. 1910. $40-60

"Gee Whiz",
Beach Haven, N.J.
c. 1912. $10-20

On the Bay, Beach Haven, N.J. c. 1908. This photograph was taken by Robert Engle and was reproduced quite heavily. The message on this card is interesting. It says "The weather here is fine and many here 'Labor Day' but numbers left to-day. Eight of us adults were in a boat like this first day going to Tuckerton (Quaker) Mtg. Got back to dinner 2:30. Our dear little girls are fine and attract much attention being dressed alike and so good and independent. They love the surf. School days soon be here. Hope thee is well thy friend, E.A. Sharpless." $4-8

Advertising card from the Engleside Hotel, Beach Haven, N.J. c. 1905. This is another photo by Robert Engle; however, this image is not as easy to find. $10-12

Racing on Barnegat Bay, N.J. c. 1925. $5-10

Sneak Box Racing on Barnegat Bay, N.J. c. 1908. Sneak boxes are a type of boat, primarily created for use in gunning. Their creation traces directly back to the shores of Barnegat Bay, N.J. $10-15

Yachting on the Bay, Beach Haven, N.J. c. 1910. "We had such a nice sail this afternoon, went clear down to the inlet." $15-20

Off For A Day's Fishing, Beach Haven, N.J. c. 1905. $8-10

Photograph, George Lee sailing on Barnegat Bay. c. 1938. $15-20

Photograph, Sailing on Barnegat Bay. c. 1939. $10-12

Bay Scene, Beach Haven, N.J. c.1938. $4-8

A Sailor's Life's the Life for Me, High Point, N.J.
c. 1910. $10-12

Sail Boat Races, Beach Haven, N.J. c. 1941. $3-6

Yachting at Beach Haven, N.J. c. 1908. $8-10

Photograph, Lifeguards and Girls on Boat, Beach Haven, N.J.
c. 1930. $8-10

View From Coast Guard Tower, Beach Haven, N.J. c. 1935. This photograph shows a number of the private docks that bayside homeowners constructed near the Bond's Coast Guard Station. This is the one-of-a-kind original photograph that the postcard would have been made from, $25-50.

Water Sports, Beach Haven, N.J. c. 1941. The sender tells Miss Claire Brackmann to "Ask Papa to tell you all he knows about Beach Haven." $4-6

Photograph, Gassing up the Speedboat, Beach Haven, N.J. c. 1938. $10-12

Returning from Moonlight Sail on Barnegat Bay, N.J. c. 1907. Going for a moonlight sail was a popular pastime in days of old. $10-15

Shadows, Beach Haven, N.J. c. 1914. $5-8

Sunset on Little Egg Harbor Bay, Long Beach Island, N.J. c. 1940. $2-5

Photograph, Sailing, Barnegat Bay. c. 1938. $12-15

137

Chapter 5
North to Brant Beach

With the establishment of Beach Haven in 1874, the idea of real estate development in other parts of the island quickly began to take off. The way it generally worked was that a development company was chartered and land was purchased. One of their first acts was to either build a hotel themselves, or entice some other investor to do it instead. A few substantial cottages would be speculatively built in close proximity to the hotel. Sometimes the names of prominent individuals would be attached to these cottages in a "look who's buying here" style of advertisement. That way, potential customers could see what awaited them in this new resort if they were lucky enough to get in on the ground floor.

A string of these types of communities, most of which were promoted by land investment companies headquartered in Philadelphia, began to pop up all over the island. The first of these continued the path of development northward from Beach Haven. This style of development would eventually, over the next eighty years, end up devouring most of the open space that was left on the island.

Waverly Beach was one of the first new communities to be created in 1884. The name of the town would eventually be changed to North Beach Haven. Today, most people just think of it as a part of Beach Haven when, in fact, it really is a part of Long Beach Township.

In addition to Waverly Beach, developers would create other small communities using the same formula. They would include Spray Beach, Beach Haven Gardens, Beach Haven Terrace, Haven Beach, Beach Haven Park, Peahala Park, Brighton Beach, and Beach Haven Crest.

The Waverly, N. Beach Haven. c. 1905. When William Hewitt, the man responsible for enticing the Pennsylvania Railroad into bringing their spur route onto the island, planned his community of Waverly Beach, now North Beach Haven, he built one hotel and had investors build another. The Waverly is the hotel that he built. His planned community never really grew beyond his dreams for it. Today this hotel is called the Hudson House, a popular local watering hole. $350

Dolphin Inn, Beach Haven, N. J.

Dolphin Inn, Beach Haven, N.J. c. 1898. The Dolphin Inn was the investor's hotel. It was built in 1887 by William Ringgold of Philadelphia and located on 13th Street in what was then Waverly Beach. It was a rather large place that sat up high on pilings, just beyond the dunes. As evidenced by this postcard, there was very little else that existed around it except for a few cottages and the Waverly Hotel, visible in the distance. $60-80

"The Breakers," North Beach Haven, N. J.
Austin & Austin

"The Breakers," North Beach Haven, N.J., Austin & Austin. c. 1913. Ringgold soon decided to start his own resort community and to build a new hotel further north on the island. So in the 1890s, he sold the Dolphin Inn to a family named Austin. They would rename it The Breakers and continue to run the old hotel until 1944. $60-80

Exchange & Parlor, The "Breakers", Beach Haven, N.J. c. 1925. This extremely rare image shows the interior of the hotel. The exchange is an antiquated term for the main lobby and front desk area of a hotel. $25-35

The "Breakers", Beach Haven, N.J. c. 1927. This close-up view of the hotel shows just how close it actually was to the real breakers, a fact that would cause great distress a few years later. A visitor at the hotel penned this card. She writes, "Am here for two weeks & like it very much. Last night it was so cold they had a great fire. This place is 6 miles out to sea. Been thinking of coming for the last four years. So cool & fine bathing. All Philadelphia people, 50 miles from Atlantic City." $160

The Breakers Hotel, North Beach Haven, N.J. c. 1935. A postcard sender writes, "At the Breaker's Hotel here, same place as I was last year. Took two weeks furlough as I had my vacation in February at Atlantic City. This is a very restful place. Good bathing. 110 miles from NY." $50-75

The Breakers Hotel, From the Dunes, Beach Haven, N.J. c. 1941. Written on the reverse, "Mr. & Mrs. Austin's place, Sept 1941." The Breakers would not be around for much longer, though. Severely undermined structurally by the Hurricane of 1944, and unable to be saved, the old hotel was torn down and the building materials were salvaged for the war effort. $50-60

Spray Beach Hotel, Spray Beach, N.J. c. 1911. When William Ringgold left Waverly Beach, it was to his new community of Spray Beach that he came. This real photo postcard shows the hotel that Ringgold built in Spray Beach in 1891 to serve as the center of activity in the community. $50-60

Spray Beach Hotel, Spray Beach, N.J. c. 1935. The old hotel would eventually be sold to Augustus Keil, and from him it would pass on through a series of owners. It was eventually demolished in 1968, after an auction of its contents. $30-50

Spray Beach, N.J. c. 1911. Ringgold also built a number of fine cottages surrounding his hotel, which is visible through the cottages in the center of the photo. John Luther Long, the man who wrote the book *Madame Butterfly,* on which the opera was based, was one of the early cottagers in Spray Beach. A number of these cottages still exist, including Long's. $20-30

Barnegat Bay. Spray Beach.
N.J. c. 1912. $8-10

Spray Beach Yacht Club, Long Beach Island, N.J. c. 1940. Located at 23rd St. & Long Beach Boulevard, the club was founded in 1922, with a primary focus on sailing. Their first clubhouse was erected in 1924. $3-6

Spray Beach Yacht Club, Spray Beach, N.J. c. 1950. $4-8

Sail Boat Races, Barnegat Bay, Spray Beach, N.J., c. 1938. $3-6

142

Spray Beach Motor Inn, Oceanfront at 24th Street, Spray Beach, N.J. c. 1970. The Spray Beach Motor Inn was built around 1970 on the site of the old Spray Beach Hotel. $3-5

Coleman's "Old Fashioned" Restaurant, Beach Haven Terrace, N.J. c. 1970. No vacation on Long Beach Island was complete without at least one meal at Coleman's. The cozy atmosphere, lit with antique lamps, was only surpassed by their fabulous seafood dinners. $6-10

Coast Guard Station, Beach Haven Terrace, N.J. c. 1920. Built in the early part of the last century, this Duluth-type life saving station now serves as a private residence. The Duluth-style stations were architecturally distinctive, with the unique placement of windows and the tower capped by a pagoda-like roof. $60-80

1635   COAST GUARD STATION,
Beach Haven Terrace, N. J.

Wagon Wheel Gift Shoppe, 11101 Long Beach Boulevard, Haven Beach, N.J. c. 1965. $6-10

Four Winds, Beach Haven Crest, N.J. c. 1935. $15-25

Chapter 6
Brant Beach

The story of Brant Beach and its promotion and development is an interesting one. Just as with so many of the other communities, it begins with a Philadelphia developer who envisioned a new community on Long Beach Island, and then set about creating it. His name was Henry McLaughlin.

McLaughlin created the Beach Haven North Company in 1909 to go about the work of promoting his new seashore resort. He intended to, and for a short while did, call it North Beach Haven. This is not to be confused with Waverly Beach, which later became North Beach Haven. In a strange twist, he decided to drop that moniker and replace it with the name Brant Beach. Possibly this was done because of a conflict with the Waverly Beach renaming situation. Whatever the case, the Brant Beach name stuck.

Brant Beach was a good choice for a name for McLaughlin's new community, given where it was situated on the island. The area around the original settlement of Brant Beach is a rather narrow section of the island with a beautifully protected cove on its bay side. The wildfowl known as brant flocked to this cove and gave McLaughlin the inspiration for renaming his new resort.

McLaughlin built a number of cottages and supplied them with a number of luxuries that were not readily available in any of the other island communities. An artesian well supplied fresh water to the community, and in the evening electricity was supplied too. In short order

McLaughlin had constructed a spacious and stylish railroad station for the patrons of his new town. It helped to project the image to newly arriving visitors, and potential customers, that this was a place of class and substance. With each trainload of visitors to Brant Beach, lots were sold and new cottages were built, making it one of the island's most attractive cottage colonies.

A second wave of development in Brant Beach would follow almost fifteen years later. In an area just to the north of the already established community, a new group of gentlemen calling themselves Brant Beach Realtors, Inc. would begin to make their mark on the island.

Following the same formula that had been created years before, one of their first actions was to build a large hotel. It was to be just the first of a number of large hotels that they proposed to construct. More construction would follow, including a movie theater. A quite lengthy boardwalk was even proposed, however it was never built.

Their grandiose plans for a major community to rival Beach Haven soon fell flat as America was plunged into the Great Depression. Small Cape Cod-style cottages became their standard of construction rather than the elaborate villas that they had hoped would populate this section of the island. Eventually street after street of these small homes would be built. In time, the two areas of Brant Beach, old and new, expanded to the point that they grew together to create the community that we are familiar with today.

Getting ready for the Saturday afternoon race – everybody sails. Barnegat Bay, Brant Beach, N.J. **c. 1912. This series of three postcards produced by McLaughlin as promotional pieces all have the same tag line on the reverse: "Send your name and address and we will forward you literature and views of Brant Beach, explaining the Brant Beach plan. Brant Beach Company, 762 North American Building, Philadelphia." This image shows just how narrow the island is at Brant Beach from the bay front to the sand dunes in the distance. Just to the left of the center boat is the Brant Beach railroad station. $20-30**

BARNEGAT BAY.   BRANT BEACH, N. J.

Boating, fishing, crabbing on a bay 4 to 6 miles wide – 40 miles long, Barnegat Bay, Brant Beach, N.J. c. 1912. $20-30

Barnegat Bay, Brant Beach, N.J. c. 1912. $20-30

Brant Beach, N.J., Pennsylvania Railroad Station. Sent July 17, 1911. On reverse: "Beach Haven North Co., Owner Brant Beach, North American Building, Philadelphia." Sent to Miss Emma Hunter, Glassboro, New Jersey: "Having a delightful time. Swell breeze. Beats Glassboro all to pieces. Friend Elsie." This handsome structure, when it had finished its useful life as a train station, was moved to the corner of Sixtieth Street in Brant Beach where it served for many years as a retail shop and later as a private residence. In 2005, local preservationists made a valiant effort to rescue this building from imminent destruction when word leaked out that it was about to be demolished to redevelop the site. A move to Beach Haven was planned, where it was to be restored and adaptively re-used. The night before it was to be moved, with all the restoration plans firmly in place, local demolition men gleefully plowed into the structure with their equipment, leveling it in minutes and horrifying those who had worked so hard to save this piece of island history. $150-170

WIDA'S HOTEL, BRANT BEACH, N.J.

Wida's Hotel, Brant Beach, N.J. c. 1932. This is the first, and only, hotel that was to be built in Brant Beach's second phase of construction. Plans were to build one large hotel every few blocks, but that never happened. Originally named the Ockanickon, it was built in 1926, and was later sold to Martin Wida in the early 1930s. $20-30

Hungarian and American Home Cooking   Open All Year   All Outside Rooms

BRANT BEACH HOTEL

WIDAS SEA FOOD RESTAURANT

Wida's Brant Beach Hotel and Silver Grill, Brant Beach, N. J.

Wida's Brant Beach Hotel, Inc. c. 1968. In recent years, Wida's remained the last of the old-style island hotels, with its huge dining room and gigantic menu. Sadly, this all came to end recently with the sale to new owners, who remodeled it into an upscale restaurant. $8-10

Wida's Brant Beach Hotel and Silver Grill, Brant Beach, N.J. c. 1935. Wida was Hungarian by birth, and so his hotel specialized in the cuisine of his homeland. The hotel was also well known for its American home-style cooking. Its Silver Grill was a popular island nightclub up until the time of World War II. $20-30

Ocean View Inn, Sam and Anna Parrish, 55th Street and Ocean Blvd., Brant Beach, N.J. June 17, 1954. This postcard depicts another of the small guesthouses that once existed on Long Beach Island. Rather than try to describe it myself, I'll let the words of the person who sent this postcard paint the picture for you: "Doesn't this remind you of B.H. House! There are no *private* baths but 2 in Annex & 3 in main house. Outside showers & 2 sun decks. They take at most 35 when full. We really think it would do nicely – not too much place for clothing – 1 closet in each room." Original Dexter Press photograph, $75-90; Postcard, $50-60.

Ocean View Inn
SAM AND ANNA PARRISH
55TH STREET AND OCEAN BLVD., BRANT BEACH, N. J.
TELEPHONES: BEACH HAVEN 4-4464, 4-4821

47409

Photograph, Camp Miquon.
c. 1939. Camp Miquon was a very exclusive camp for boys, which was located on the oceanfront, between 56th and 58th Streets, in Brant Beach. It operated from 1924 to 1940 and its last vestiges were wiped clear by the Hurricane of 1944. $20-30

Photograph, Brant Beach looking West from 56th Street. c. 1939. This photograph, and the five that follow, come from an album prepared by Mr. & Mrs. C. Edgar Marvin, Jr., of Glenside, Pennsylvania, that documents the construction of their new vacation home on 56th Street in Brant Beach. They began to take photos the day construction was about to begin on the house in 1938 and followed the progress to completion, and after, through new pets, a world war, and the Hurricane of 1944. They named their summer place the Fo'c'sle. In this picture, looking across Brant Beach to the bay, there is almost nothing visible except for a sign for the Ocean View House located one block away. The home that they built was typical of the small cottages that began to populate all of the streets in this section of the island. Photo album value, $560.

Photograph, The Fo'c'sle, 56th Street, Brant Beach. c. 1939. The Marvins' home still stands today, looking very much as it did when they built it. Increasingly, though, these small cottages are under threat of demolition as developers look at them for their lots as places to build super-sized monstrosities.

148

Photograph, Hurricane (9.14.44) Damage, The Fo'c'sle & Neighbors – 10/14/44. **One month to the day after the September hurricane of 1944, and the damage is still evident on 56th Street. What looks like the aftermath of a snowstorm is actually the sand that remains in the street. The force of the storm toppled the neighbor's chimney. All in all, this damage was mild in comparison to what some properties suffered.**

Photograph, Pepper, The New Puppy, May 1942, The Fo'c'sle, Brant Beach, N.J. c. 1942.

Photograph, Scott's. **c. 1944. This home on the ocean end of 56th Street lost its garage door, and the apron into the garage appears to have dropped into a hole.**

Photograph, Beach-Front Property. c. 1944. This photo was taken somewhere in the vicinity of the Marvin home, most likely at the end of 56th Street on the ocean. It truly shows the power of the destructive forces of nature.

Municipal Building, Brant Beach, N.J. c. 1935. $3-5

Lucille's Own Make Candies, Boulevard and 41st St., Brant Beach, Long Beach Island, N.J. c. 1965. Lucille's has long been a landmark in Brant Beach with its giant-sized piece of salt-water taffy outside. $6-8

The Evangelical Lutheran Church of the Holy Trinity, Brant Beach, N.J. c. 1960. This congregation was first organized in 1940, and the building was built and dedicated in 1956. The church looks very much the same today, except for its current Lutheran-Red paint scheme. $3-5

St. Francis Church, Long Beach Island. c. 1960. **This church building was built in 1958 to handle the growing population of Catholics on the island. The two Catholic churches in Beach Haven and Surf City were no longer sufficient. Since then an entire complex of buildings known as the St. Francis Center has sprung up around the church to serve the needs of Catholics, and also non-Catholics, on Long Beach Island. $3-5**

Interior, Church of St. Francis of Assisi, 46th St. & Boulevard, Brant Beach, N.J. c. 1960. $3-5

Chapter 7
Ship Bottom – Beach Arlington

Just as the vast open spaces between Beach Haven and Brant Beach developed into a number of small communities, so too did the section of the island that we know today as Ship Bottom. Unlike those communities that just sort of melted away into one long stretch of homes that are today part of Long Beach Township, these small communities banded together to became one large self-governing community.

Today most people think that Ship Bottom got its name from the shipwreck on its beach that graces the borough logo, the wreck of *The Fortuna*. This Italian barque ran aground at Ship Bottom's Sixteenth Street beach in January of 1910. That, however, is not the origin of the name. According to Charles Edgar Nash in his 1937 edition of *The Lure of Long Beach*, a clipper crashed into the shores of the island around the year 1817, and that was the wreck from which the community known as Ship Bottom actually got its name.

Apparently Captain Stephen Willets, a man strong in faith and trusting of spiritual guidance, felt the urge to go to sea in the aftermath of a great storm. There was something telling him that there was a ship in distress that needed his help. As he sailed the length of Long Beach Island, there was nothing that appeared out of the ordinary to him or his crew. Still sensing that something was wrong, he urged his crew closer and precariously closer to shore, eventually setting off in just a small boat.

Just as they were about to give up, the hull of a capsized ship loomed up before them. From within the ship they could hear a faint tapping. Seizing an axe they chopped their way through the hull and pulled out into the daylight a young woman who spoke to them in a foreign tongue. There were no other survivors of the wreck.

They rowed the young survivor to shore and to the safety that only dry land can provide. Dropping to her knees there on that beach she drew the sign of the cross in the sand. From that day forward the section of beach where she drew that cross has been known as Ship Bottom. And what became of the young woman? She was supposedly assisted in making her way from the area, never to return.

Ship Bottom, New Jersey.
c. 1965. $5-10

The spot upon which she drew the cross, and which was thereafter know as Ship Bottom, technically only consisted of the five blocks that today are the five most southern blocks of the town. These blocks were centered on the Ship Bottom Life Saving Station. North of these five blocks extended the other small communities that would ultimately combine to become the Ship Bottom that we know today.

Those other communities are places that most people have never heard of. They had names like Beach Arlington, Bonnet Beach, Bonnie Beach, and Edgewater Beach. Beach Arlington was the largest of these communities,

and so in 1925 when they all merged, it was decided that the name of the community created was to be Ship Bottom–Beach Arlington.

The real reason for this strange name probably had to do with the fact that the United States Life Saving Station was named Ship Bottom Life Saving Station, yet the Pennsylvania Railroad stop for the town was on maps as Beach Arlington. The combined name kept the town from having to wrangle with either the government or the railroad. In time, though, the railroad would disappear from the island, and so too would the Beach Arlington name.

Ship Bottom, N.J. c. 1960. It is remarkable to note just how much vacant land still existed in Ship Bottom fifty years ago. $5-10

Comic Card, Ship Bottom. c. 1921. $8-12

Wreck of the Barque "Fortuna" near Beach Haven, N.J. c. 1910. The steel-hulled Italian barque *Fortuna* made headlines when she crashed into the beach in Ship Bottom, N.J. in January of 1910. Everyone on board the ship was safely rescued, but the *Fortuna* was not as lucky. $30-60

Fortuna, Trapani. c. 1910. The *Fortuna* rolled into the surf after standing upright for four days. People came from far and wide to view the wreck and to be photographed standing next to it. Eventually she was dismantled for salvage. Postcards were produced to document the wreck and sold for quite some time afterwards, as evidenced by this card, mailed from Beach Haven almost nine months after the event. $80-100

Railroad Station, Ship Bottom-Beach Arlington, N.J. c. 1925. This was a rather small, unadorned station in comparison to those at either end of the island. It was located at 23rd Street in Ship Bottom, across from Conrad Brothers Lumber Company. $50-70

460   Railroad Station, Ship Bottom-Beach Arlington, N. J.

Ship Bottom Municipal Building, Ship Bottom, N.J. c. 1950. $3-6

Fire House, Ship Bottom-Beach Arlington, N.J. c. 1925. Given the island's history with fire, it is no wonder that volunteer fire companies were started in most of her communities. This station in Ship Bottom was a classic bit of shore architecture, combining design elements of the Brant Beach Train Station with the old Life Saving Stations to come up with its look. $130

013   Fire House, Ship Bottom-Beach Arlington, N. J.

U.S. Coast Guard Station, Ship Bottom-Beach Arlington, N.J. c. 1940. The Life Saving Station in Ship Bottom was different in design from any of the others on LBI. It was a Jersey pattern-type station design. The surfmen of this station were a much decorated group, having won seven gold medals for one 1903 rescue alone. $5-10

U. S. Coast Guard Station, Ship Bottom-Beach, Arlington, N. J.

ON THE WAVES
18TH STREET AND OCEAN, SHIP BOTTOM, N. J.

22249

On The Waves, 18th and Ocean, Ship Bottom, N.J. c.1935. Ship Bottom did not have the large hotels, like those that were available in Beach Haven. Instead, there were a number of oceanfront guest cottages, like this one, that served the needs of visitors to the town. This is a Dexter Press original photo from which the postcard would have been made, $55.

Camp Dune By-the-Sea
Ship Bottom, Beach Arlington, N. J.

Camp Dune By-the-Sea, Ship Bottom-Beach Arlington, N.J. c. 1935. This was an exclusive camp for girls, run by the daughter of the Mayor of Ship Bottom. It was located on the beach between 25th and 26th Streets. In later years it was operated as the Dunes Hotel. It was demolished in the 1970s. $10-15

Drifting Sands Motel, 8th St. at the Ocean, Ship Bottom, N.J. c. 1965. $3-6

Grant's Motel, Central Avenue between 18th and 19th Streets, Ship Bottom, New Jersey. c. 1965. $4-8

Islander Motel, 12th and Central Ave., Ship Bottom, N.J. c. 1975. $2-5

Ship Bottom Motor Lodge, Ship Bottom, N.J. c. 1975. **Take note of the use of the image of the wreck of the** *Fortuna* **on the sign at the Motor Lodge. $2-5**

Photograph, Long Beach Boulevard, Ship Bottom. **c. 1935. This image is taken in front of the former garage building that for many years has been the home of the Long Beach Candy Company. The building in the distance is the Hotel Elton, another of Ship Bottom's small guesthouses. $90**

Chris' Garage, Ship Bottom, N.J. c. 1934. $145

CHRIS' GARAGE, SHIP BOTTOM, N. J.

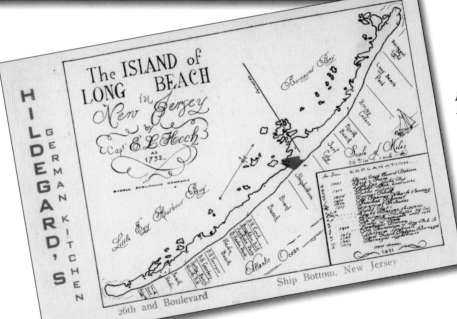

Hildegard's German Kitchen, 26th and Boulevard, Ship Bottom, N.J. c. 1955. $10-15

The Blue Room, Beach Arlington, N.J. c. 1935. Very little is known about this establishment, other than that they advertised themselves as "South Jersey's Smartest Cabaret Restaurant." It certainly looks like it was a rather swanky place, with its Art Deco décor and nautical motif. $20

Mecleary's Shore Bar and Restaurant, 20th & Boulevard, Ship Bottom, N.J. c. 1955. They billed the place as New Jersey's Largest Bar "on Long Beach Island six miles at sea." In later years Mecleary's would become Joe Pop's Shore Bar. $10-20

Jack's De Luxe Diner, Ship Bottom, N.J. c. 1950. "Specializing in sea foods cooked to order. Anything from a sandwich to a full course meal." $10-20

JACK'S DE LUXE DINER

Ship Bottom, New Jersey

Stutz Candy Company, Bay Ave. at 14th St., Ship Bottom, Long Beach Island, N.J. c. 1960. This wonderful candy store still retains much of the same charm today, and their candy is great! $3-6

Birds-eye View, Ship Bottom, N.J. c. 1950.
Ship Bottom was primarily a community
of small bungalow-style cottages. Street
after street was filled with these charming,
affordable vacation homes. Today these
historic cottages are being demolished,
one after another, to make room for utterly
charmless structures that would be more
appropriate in some boring suburban development, not on Long Beach Island. $6-10

*Photograph, Oceanfront
Cottages, 25th Street, Ship
Bottom, N.J. c. 1930.* A
postcard sender wrote
from the island: "It is all
right here at the shore but
this is the dampest place I
have ever been in. I think
my friend was crazy to put
$1800 in this wonderful
cottage here!" $30-50

*Photograph, Bayside
Cottages, Address Unknown,
Ship Bottom, N.J. c. 1930.*
These cottages are typical of
the type built in Ship Bottom
in the 1920s. A small dock juts
into the bay from in front of
the end house. The writing on
the back says, "Chas's is the
neatest looking one." $45-60

160

1390   Cottages Along the Boulevard, Ship Bottom, N. J.

Cottages Along the Boulevard, Ship Bottom, N.J. c. 1925. This row of cottages, though not in the greatest of locations adjacent to the railroad tracks, was constructed in a somewhat more substantial style than most of the cottages in Ship Bottom. Located across the street from the Hand Store in Ship Bottom, and used as their Garden Center, the last of these cottages was torn down in 2006. $100-115

View looking South. Ship Bottom. N. J.

View Looking South, Ship Bottom, N.J. c. 1935. $8-12

Horseshoe Point, Ship Bottom, N.J. c. 1941. By the late 1930s, more substantial cottages were beginning to be built in most of the developing areas of the island. Ship Bottom was no exception. $10-20

HORSESHOE POINT, SHIPBOTTOM, N. J.

Private Cottages Along The Ocean, Ship Bottom, N.J. c. 1941. The sender of this postcard writes, "Some of the homes of Haddonfield people, Mrs. Irving, Mr. & Mrs. Clark, and Robertson." $10-15

THE BUSTER BROWN COTTAGE, SHIPBOTTOM, N. J.

The Buster Brown Cottage, Ship Bottom, N.J. c. 1944. It is not clear just what the meaning of this postcard is; however, it is thought that it refers to the owner of the cottage and not the cartoon character of the same name! $30-40

Union Chapel of Beach Arlington, N.J. c. 1925. This nondenominational chapel was built in 1924 and was the first church in Ship Bottom. For years prior to its construction, Sunday morning services were conducted in the town's railroad station. This image was taken shortly after the chapel was built. $15-20

1391   Union Chapel of Beach Arlington, N. J.

162

Union Church. Ship Bottom-Beach. Arlington, N. J.

Union Chapel, Ship Bottom-Beach Arlington, N.J. c. 1943. $7-10

Hello Aunt Pink

SAND DUNES, Ship Bottom, N. J.

Sand Dunes, Ship Bottom, N.J. c. 1924. "Dear Aunt Pink, You certainly did touch the spot with that 'dolla'. I sure do appreciate it. Thus far I have been unable to swallow the sea – but almost – Archie." $6-8

Bathing Beach, Ship Bottom, N. J.

Bathing Beach, Ship Bottom, N.J. c. 1935. $5-7

163

Beach Scene, Ship Bottom-Beach Arlington, N.J. c. 1935. Even postcard publishers are not above making mistakes! This is the Dexter Press photograph that was used to make a postcard of a beach scene in Ship Bottom. It's obvious that this is not Ship Bottom, with its boardwalk and amusement places. In reality it is Seaside Heights. The back of the photo had instructions stating that this should be cropped out of the image on the postcard, but a look at the postcard shows that that was never done. Photograph, $15-20; Postcard, $7-10.

On the Beach, Ship Bottom-Beach Arlington, N.J. c.1935. $7-10

Enjoying the Beach and Sun at Ship Bottom, N.J. c. 1940. $5-8

Fishing Pier, Beach Arlington, Ship Bottom, N.J. c. 1935. Just as in Beach Haven, Ship Bottom had its own municipal fishing pier. And just as in Beach Haven, it was washed away in the 1944 hurricane. Original Dexter Press photo from which the postcard would have been made, $15-20.

FISHING PIER
Beach Arlington, Ship Bottom, N. J.

4382

PUBLIC DOCK, SHIP BOTTOM

Public Dock, Ship Bottom, N.J. c.1940. Swimming in the bay, and the bay beaches, is often preferred by families with children since the waters are calmer and not as dangerous. $10-15

Boat Dock on the Bay, Ship Bottom – Beach Arlington, N.J. c. 1935. Original postcard photo, $15-20.

7086

Boat Dock on the Bay
Ship Bottom - Beach Arlington, N. J.

Bay Front, Ship Bottom, N. J.

Bay Front, Ship Bottom, N.J. c. 1940. $5-7

Chapter 8
The Pound Fishermen

At one time commercial fishing was, in addition to tourism, one of the major economic engines that drove Long Beach Island's commerce. At its peak there were five different fisheries operating on the island. And of these five, all fished the waters off LBI by the pound fishing method.

Pound fishing is a system whereby large poles are driven into the ocean floor and nets are attached to them. At the end of the pound is a heart-shaped fore bay which leads to a trap, or pocket. These pounds were generally placed at a depth of between thirty-five and fifty feet. The way it worked was that schools of fish swimming along from either direction would encounter the pound, which was generally up to 1500 feet in length. Once encountered, they swam along its netting in an effort to get around it; being channeled into the fore bay, and then into the pocket. There they ended up trapped.

The pound fisherman would check their nets daily by hauling up these pockets. From these nets would then be culled the fish that were commercially saleable, while others were tossed back into the ocean. In the days before environmental consciousness, oddities such as sharks and sea turtles were captured which were often hauled in as trophies to be displayed at the fisheries and posed with for photographs.

The Long Beach Island pound fishermen, mainly of Norwegian, Danish, and Swedish ancestry, were almost as much of a tourist attraction as were the beaches. People would flock around as the large pound boats were dramatically landed on the beach, brimming full with their daily catch. The fish that were captured in the pounds were then taken to the fisheries and sorted, packed in barrels of ice, and transported to the fish markets of New York City where they were then sold.

For a great many years this was a very successful operation, but one by one the pound fisheries began to falter and to close. The hurricane of 1944 was very costly to the fisheries. It caused great damage to the nets and poles that made up the pounds. And at the same time there was a war that was raging in the Atlantic that many felt severely impacted her ecosystem, in turn causing a substantial drop in the amount of fish appearing in the waters along the shore of New Jersey. Profitability of the commercial fisheries was dramatically impacted by this, leading to further closures. By 1957, the last of Long Beach Island's pound fisheries had disappeared.

Repairing Fish Pounds, Long Beach Island, N.J. c. 1939. $20-30

Real Photo Postcard of Pound Fisherman Landing Their Boats. c. 1935. $200

Fishing Boat Cresting a Breaking Wave — Long Beach Island, N. J.

Fishing Boat Cresting a Breaking Wave, Long Beach Island, N.J. c. 1938. $10-15

8-36   Fishing Boats   Ship Bottom-Beach, Arlington, N. J.

Fishing Boats, Ship Bottom-Beach Arlington, N.J. c. 1925. $40-50

Photograph, Pound Fishing Boats and Horse. c. 1935. $80-90

Return of the Fishing Boats in Surf, Long Beach Island, N.J. c. 1940. On the reverse of a pound fishing post-card, the caption reads: "Romantic Fishing Boats – The early morning landings of the colorful fishing skiffs on the beaches of magic Long Beach Island are a wonderful sight! The men are hardy Norsemen and they produce vitamin rich fish food for the nation." $10-15

Chapter 9
From the Mainland to the Island

As mentioned in a previous chapter, the earliest means of conveyance of passengers across the bay to Long Beach Island was by sail. The stage, and later the railroad, could bring you to the shores of the mainland in either Tuckerton or Barnegat, but it still required a boat of some type to get you to the island.

That changed when the Pennsylvania Railroad built its much-anticipated connection to Long Beach Island. Trains were finally able to make their way over onto LBI by way of a mile-long wooden trestle, replete with drawbridge. It was constructed across Manahawkin Bay from Manahawkin on the mainland to Ship Bottom on the island, by way of the Bonnet islands. From there it could head in either direction, north to Barnegat City or south to Beach Haven.

For years, the trains would be the quickest and most viable way to get to the island. That was all about to change when an idea was floated to create a turnpike company that would build an automobile causeway across the bay and onto the island. This was a pretty forward-thinking idea when it was put forth in 1912, given that nothing remotely akin to Long Beach Boulevard even existed on the island. But that didn't stop the investors of the Long Beach Turnpike Company from proceeding with their plans to build a bridge and also a boulevard.

While the causeway was being built, work was also underway to create Long Beach Boulevard. On June 20, 1914, the new wood-planked causeway, which ran parallel to the old railroad trestle, opened to automobile traffic. A huge parade of cars, all gaily decorated for the occasion, and led by New Jersey's Governor James F. Fielder, made their way across the causeway and then on to Beach Haven on the newly completed boulevard. It may not have been apparent to the participants then, but on that day, the death knell had begun to ring for the island's rail passenger service.

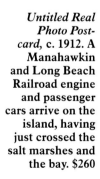

Untitled Real Photo Postcard, c. 1912. A Manahawkin and Long Beach Railroad engine and passenger cars arrive on the island, having just crossed the salt marshes and the bay. $260

Two Mile Automobile Bridge over Little Egg Harbor Bay, Beach Haven, N.J. c. 1916. The opening of this wood-planked causeway created quite a stir on the island. Its completion ushered in a new area of development on LBI. $125

Auto Bridge near Beach Haven, N.J. c. 1925. Although the bridge was miles away from Beach Haven, local stores that sold postcards didn't hesitate to market it as though it was a direct improvement to the town. $100-115

The Causeway Across Barnegat Bay. c. 1940. "Poor Ink, Poor Pen, Poor Writer, Amen!" $60-80

Real Photo Postcard of the Causeway Bridge. c. 1948. A postcard can sometimes be dated by the postmark on the card, but rarely can you pinpoint the exact moment when the photo was taken. That is not the case with this card, postmarked September 21, 1948, and sent to Mr. Bob Mott in Tuckerton, New Jersey. The photographer just happened to be Bill Kane, owner of the Nor'easter Store in Beach Haven Terrace, and on the card he writes, "How do you like this snap of the bridge? I took it last Sunday morning." $75-100

Draw-bridge Entrance to Long Beach Island, N.J. c. 1950. This image shows the draw-bridge portion of the old causeway. It was a bascule-style bridge. $15-30

Causeway Bridge Entering Ship Bottom – Beach Arlington, N.J. c. 1930. Original photograph from which Dexter Press produced the postcard. Photo, $65; Postcard of same image, $10-15.

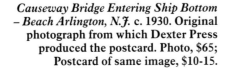

Long Beach Island Causeway. c. 1965. In the late 1950s, it was decided to replace the old causeway with a new, modern causeway that could accommodate the extra traffic coming onto the island, and at the same time get rid of the interminable backups created by the drawbridge. The new bridge would hop-scotch across the bay by way of the Bonnet Islands. $3-6

View of the Causeway, Ship Bottom, N.J. c. 1964. $3-6

Causeway Bridge, Ship Bottom, N.J. c. 1960. $3-6

The Dutchman's Brau Haus, Long Beach Island Causeway, N.J. c. 1965. The Dutchman's Brau Haus is located on Cedar Bonnet Island. The original restaurant building sat directly adjacent to the old Causeway. It has been run by the Schmid family since it was first opened in 1952. The building pictured on this postcard was built in 1965. $4-6

Gateway to Ship Bottom. c. 1948. $60-80

The Dutchman's Brau Haus, Long Beach Island Causeway, N.J. c. 1972. This great interior view shows three different areas within the Dutchman restaurant. The place has an authentic German feel to it and their sauerbraten is the best to be had anywhere! $2-4

Traffic Circle, Entrance to Long Beach Island, N.J. c. 1940. On the reverse: "The modern traffic circle is the entrance to the six happy, healthy family resorts of Long Beach Island." $4-6

Chapter 10
Surf City

The community of Surf City has deep roots on Long Beach Island; roots that go deeper than any of the island's other communities. Some of her earliest settlers, who arrived prior to 1700, were the men who came with their families to establish a whaling station at what is considered to be the easternmost point of Long Beach Island. Descendants of this group of early families still remain in the vicinity of the island today.

In the early days, this section of the Island was known as Great Swamp. At one time it had grown thick with white cedar, but legend has it that a coastal hurricane wiped out much of this growth. It is said that sometimes, after great storms, the stumps of these trees lie exposed in the surf and on the beaches of Surf City.

At the same time that the first hotel was being built in what is today Holgate at the southern end of the island, a real estate group was put together to build a hotel at Great Swamp. The hotel at the south end was the Philadelphia Company House, later known as Bond's Long Beach House. The hotel built at Great Swamp was called the Mansion of Health, playing on the concept of the healthful qualities of the island and the sea air.

Built in 1821, on the bay side of the island, this hotel was one of the earliest hotels at the Jersey Shore to capitalize on the idea of sea bathing and beach vacations. For a great many years it did a booming business, even though it was an arduous journey to get there. Unfor-tunately, with the arrival of a railroad to Atlantic City in 1854 and the accompanying ease and convenience of getting there, the resort that had developed around the Mansion of Health went into decline. It would take the coming of a railroad to Long Beach Island in 1886 to resuscitate the flagging fortunes of what had by then been renamed Long Beach City.

The old Mansion of Health, which many thought to be haunted, had become derelict and finally burned to the ground in 1874. A smaller version of the old place was then built on the foundations of the burned hotel. With the arrival of the railroad, its owners, sensing that the action was going to be centered on the ocean and not on the bay, moved the new Mansion House to a spot much closer to the beach. Ownership would change through the years, and each change would bring a change of name to the establishment. The Mansion House would yield to the Long Beach Inn, which in turn would become the Marquette Hotel.

In 1894, after confusing the United States Postal Service for long enough because of the similarity of its name with Long Branch, New Jersey, the community that until then was known as Long Beach City changed its name one more time. This time community leaders chose the name Surf City for their little town. It is a name that has finally managed to last. And the Marquette Hotel became the Surf City Hotel.

Surf City Hotel, W. E. Searl, Proprietor, Boulevard at 8th Street, Between Ocean and Barnegat Bay. c. 1923. **Searl purchased the old Marquette Hotel from its previous owner and changed its name to the Surf City Hotel, a name it retains to this day. $40-50**

SURF CITY HOTEL, W. E. SEARL, Proprietor
Boulevard at 8th Street—Between Ocean and Barnegat Bay

Surf City Hotel, Surf City, N.J. c. 1948. Contained within the walls of this building is the structure of the 1884 Mansion Hotel from the days when Surf City was known as Long Beach City. $20-30

Surf City Hotel, 8th and Boulevard, Surf City, N.J. c. 1946. In 1946, George Bowles and brothers Frank and Bill Mayo purchased the Surf City Hotel. A huge number of improvements were made to the building and to the restaurant including new bars and, in 1952, the installation of a giant Wurlitzer theater organ. $15-25

Surf City Hotel, The Organ Spot of the World, Surf City, N.J. c. 1967. Take note of the image of the hotel's bar in the lower right corner of this postcard. The "Mighty Wurlitzer," as this postcard refers to the hotel's theater organ, had its console installed in the center of the bar. Through windows in the sidewall of the barroom, patrons could watch the inner workings of the great organ, as a host of celebrated organists played the organ nightly. $4-8

Surf Villa, Surf City, N.J. c. 1939. Built in 1927 at 16th Street and the Boulevard, the Surf Villa was considered a high-class establishment for the shore. It survived Prohibition and received one of the first liquor licenses to be handed out in town when Prohibition was repealed. $60-$80

Bill's Restaurant, Division Street & Boulevard, Surf City, N.J. c. 1960. A popular dining establishment in Surf City, Bill's advertised on its postcard that it had "excellent food" and a "pleasant atmosphere." $3-7

George's Italian-American Restaurant, 11th & Boulevard, Surf City, N.J. c. 1965. "Where Dining is Always A Pleasure." $3-7

POST OFFICE, SURF CITY, N. J.

Post Office, Surf City, N.J. c. 1945. Surf City was a sparsely populated place for much of its history. There were a few large Victorian homes, but little else. Most of these homes have since been destroyed, either by man or by nature, like the one pictured here. In the early days of the U.S. Postal Service, post offices were often run out of the home of the person who happened to be the town's postmaster, as was most likely the case with this home in Surf City. $20-30

CATHOLIC CHURCH
Beach Arlington, Ship Bottom, N. J.

Catholic Church, Beach Arlington, Ship Bottom, N.J. c. 1940. Another example of a postcard mistake! This is actually the old St. Thomas of Villanova Catholic Chapel, which was built in Surf City in 1898. $10-15

The United Church of Surf City, N.J. c. 1965. The reverse of the card indicates that this is an interdenominational church that conducts service in June, July, August, and September. It bills itself as "Your Vacation Church." $3-7

177

Scene Around Surf City, N.J. c. 1942. "Guess this will have to do for a Birthday Greeting. I guess no one has birthdays in Surf City, couldn't find a card. It is still warm and close here and the sun still shines. Sincerely, Harley & Mabel." $5-8

Beach and Cottages Along the Shore, Surf City, N.J. c. 1959. These cottages are typical of the style of structure that proliferated along the beaches of LBI in the 1950s and '60s. What is not typical is the empty beach! $3-7

Greetings From Surf City, N.J. c. 1939. "How would you like to take a trip on one of these boats? We want Aunt Mame to go out but she is just a little afraid." $8-12

Taking the boats out of the water after a day of racing, from the Surf City Yacht Club.
c. 1965. $2-4

Sail Boats At Yacht Club, Surf City, N.J. c. 1957. $4-6

Chapter 11
Harvey Cedars & Loveladies

Long Beach Island, many argue, is, and has always been, like two different places – the south end of the island and the north end of the island. I personally find it is more like three. Smack in the middle, dividing the north from the south, are Ship Bottom and Surf City, both of which have a similar flavor and style that is completely different from either of the island's ends.

Nowhere on the island is the difference of place more physically evident than the minute one passes the boundary of Surf City and starts to head north into Long Beach Township territory. Entering into the old Frazier Tract, which is today North Beach, on the way to Harvey Cedars, Loveladies, and Barnegat Light, it becomes quite apparent that you have entered a different section of the island. It is a wilder, more wide-open place.

For the most part, it has always been like this on the island's north end. Except for Barnegat City at the Island's northern tip, and a few other pockets of construction, much of the land north of Surf City lay undeveloped for years. Access to these areas was quite limited. What few roads existed were barely passable. Steamboats connected the large hotels of Barnegat City with the mainland; however the vast open areas to the south would only begin to see limited development with the arrival of the railroad in the late 1880s.

One of these pockets of development was at a place called Harvey Cedars. There on a small bay island, or hummock, right off the shore of the island, the Harvey Cedars Hotel was established. It had begun life as a private home sometime after 1800, but under a succession of owners the home was expanded, and it continued to grow, until it became one of the finest hotels at the Jersey Shore.

Present day Harvey Cedars is actually made up of two separate areas of land. The first is the area that was historically known as Harvey Cedars. This was a large section of land that was centered upon the Harvey Cedars Life Saving Station and the Harvey Cedars Hotel. The Harvey Cedars Beach Company mapped out this land in 1886. Streets were planned that were named after the counties of New Jersey. Today the area between Bergen and Sussex Avenues equates to the property of the Harvey Cedars Beach Company.

The other area of land consisted of two large parcels of property that were owned by Isaac Lee and Josiah Kinsey. Lee owned the southern fifty acres of the parcel, while Kinsey owned the northern one hundred acres. The combined parcel stretched north from Sussex Avenue all the way to 87th Street. Lee and Kinsey would name their settlement High Point. They would aggressively begin to develop this community by building a hotel, a yacht club, and a number of small- to moderate-sized cottages that could be rented out. Lee would also build a substantial home for himself, located on what is now Lee Avenue, and Kinsey would build a general store.

The extension north of Long Beach Boulevard brought growth and change to the two settlements. Ultimately, as the two grew and merged into one single community, High Point emerged as the combined area's center of activity. However, when the Post Office forced the dropping of one of the two identities, Harvey Cedars, the more historic of the two names, emerged as the winner.

SIDE VIEW, HARVEY CEDARS HOTEL

Side View, Harvey Cedars Hotel. c. 1915. Originally built as a private home by Sylvanus Cox, it was later sold to Samuel Perrine, who greatly expanded the place and called it the Connahassatt House. When Perrine died, the hotel was sold to Isaac Jennings, who ran it as the Harvey Cedars Hotel. Jennings would go on to become the first Mayor of Harvey Cedars. The final person to run the place as a hotel was Daniel Frazier. $15-20

Camp Whelen, Harvey Cedars, N. J.

Camp Whelan, Harvey Cedars, N.J., c. 1925. In 1921, the Philadelphia YWCA bought the old hotel from Frazier as a place for young career girls from the city to get away and have some fun. The Great Depression brought an end to the fun times at Camp Whelan. Those fortunate enough to have jobs were more concerned with keeping them than spending time at the beach. The Camp closed for good in 1935 and would sit empty for almost six years. $15-20

The Veranda, Camp Whelan, Harvey Cedars, N.J. c. 1930. "Hello Emma, am spending my vacation here at this Y.W.C.A. camp. It is on Barnegat Bay and a five-minute walk from the ocean. An ideal place to rest." $10-15

Sailing at Camp Whelan, Harvey Cedars, N.J. July 10, 1933. Sent to Mr. & Mrs. Russell Briant, Haddonfield N.J. "Dear Dennia & Russell, I Think I Told you that I would be at camp for the month of July. Watch the papers for advertising of Camp Whelan. I hope you are having a pleasant summer. Elizabeth Myers." $8-12

Harvey Cedars Bible Conference By The Sea, Harvey Cedars, New Jersey. c. 1955. In 1941, Jack Murray, a leader in the "Summer Bible School" movement, discovered the old Harvey Cedars Hotel sitting vacant. He thought it would make a great permanent home for the summer students of the program and proceeded to raise the funds to buy the old place. Rechristened The Harvey Cedars Bible Conference, its ministry is interdenominational. Today, over 15,000 people a year participate in the ongoing ministry of the Bible Conference. $3-5

Dorothy Krauss Memorial Prayer Tower, Harvey Cedars Bible Conference, Harvey Cedars, New Jersey. c. 1948. Probably the most distinctive feature of the old Harvey Cedars Hotel was its central tower. This seems to have been an architectural feature that was quite popular on Victorian seashore hotels. $6-8

Harvey Cedars Bible Conference. c. 1965. Taken from the air, this view shows the much-expanded hummock, now connected by a bridge to the island, upon which the hotel was built. $4-7

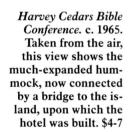

Sunset on Peaceful Barnegat Bay, Harvey Cedars Bible Conference, Harvey Cedars, New Jersey. c. 1947. $3-5

183

Long Beach Island Fishing Club, Harvey Cedars, New Jersey. c. 1950. On the reverse: "The Long Beach Island Fishing Club building is the site of the first United States Coast Guard Station. From its tower can be seen the beautiful Atlantic Ocean and Barnegat Bay. This Club sponsors annually the 'World Series' Invitation Inter-Club Surf Fishing Tournament." The original settlement of Harvey Cedars was centered upon the Hotel and the life saving station. This later station structure, referred to as a Duluth-type station, was purchased by the fishing club when it was decommissioned. $15-20

Street Scene, High Point, N. J.   Published by J. B. Kinsey.

Street Scene, High Point, N.J. c. 1908. Looking towards the bay on what was then 74th Street in High Point, and is today Lee Avenue in Harvey Cedars. The homes that line the street are typical of the small cottages built by Kinsey and Lee that could be rented by vacationers coming to their new town. $135

Lee Avenue and the High Point Inn. c. 1909. This real photo postcard again shows what is today Lee Avenue, looking towards Barnegat Bay. The mansard-roofed building in the center of the photo is the High Point Inn. This structure would burn to the ground in 1914. $100-150

Birdseye View of High Point, N.J. c. 1908. Looking north towards Love-ladies, this view was most likely taken from the roof of the High Point Inn. In the foreground is the home of Isaac Lee, one of the founders of High Point, on what is now Lee Avenue. $50-60

Birdseye View View of High Point, N. J.   Published by J. B. Kinsey

High Point Yacht Club and Landing, High Point, N. J.   Published by J. B. Kinsey.

High Point Yacht Club and Landing, High Point, N.J. c. 1908. Located on the bay at 78th Street in High Point, it was later sold and converted to a private residence. $20-30

Main Road Through High Point, N.J. c. 1925. Today we know this as Long Beach Boulevard in Harvey Cedars. This building, which served as High Point's Post Office, was located on the Boulevard at the end of Lee Avenue. Notice on the left the train tracks with a boxcar sitting on them. $70-90

1643   MAIN ROAD THROUGH High Point, N. J.

€41   General Store, High Point, N. J.

General Store, High Point, N.J. c. 1925. Originally built by J.B. Kinsey around 1910, the store would later be sold to John Maskell. General stores like this were the hub of much activity in small resort towns. They provided you with all the supplies you needed to survive your stay, and also sold the gas you needed to run your car, as witnessed by the old globe-top gas pump in front of the store. Later this business would be owned by Sam Lear, who would produce and sell at his store a great number of the postcards of High Point and Harvey Cedars. $60-75

Sand Dunes, High Point, N.J. c. 1925. $4-6

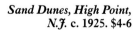
SAND DUNES, High Point, N. J.—Pub. for J. B. Kinsey

Bathing Scene in High Point, N.J. c. 1925. $10-15

The Ship's Wheel Gift Shop and Post Office, Harvey Cedars, N.J. c. 1950. As the town grew, more businesses were added. The Ship's Wheel, which sold toys, notions, gifts, and novelties, also did double duty as the town's post office. This building would be destroyed in the Northeaster of 1962. $25-30

Neptune Bar & Package Store, Harvey Cedars, N.J. c. 1950. This building began life as the Neptune Dining Room, a typical Jersey Shore seafood restaurant. By the time this postcard was made, the building had been expanded and converted to Nic Lion's Neptune Bar & Package Store. $35-45

View from Gift Shop, Looking North, Harvey Cedars, N.J. c. 1950. $20-30

Looking North Towards Barnegat Light, N.J. c. 1940. $10-15

Looking South from Harvey Cedars, New Jersey. c. 1942. Emmit S. Ramsay writes to his friend Dr. E. L. Drake in Philadelphia, Pennsylvania, telling him of the wartime activity off the island: "Dear Drakes, Sorry I have to ditch the appointment for the 22nd. Conditions here unfavorable. Will try to have our crowd down later in the season. Plenty of activity along the coast." $5-10

A PRIVATE COTTAGE, HARVEY CEDARS, N. J.

A Private Cottage, Harvey Cedars, N.J. c. 1940. The large oceanside home pictured on this postcard belonged to Frederick P. Small, the President of American Express. Mr. Small owned a huge tract of land that stretched from the ocean to the bay, upon which he had erected a variety of structures. This home would be destroyed in the Northeaster of 1962. $10-15

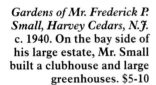

Gardens of Mr. Frederick P. Small, Harvey Cedars, N.J. c. 1940. On the bay side of his large estate, Mr. Small built a clubhouse and large greenhouses. $5-10

Wind Mill & Flower Gardens of Mr. Frederick P. Small, Harvey Cedars, N.J. c. 1951. $5-10

St. Vincent's – Main Dining Room, Sisters of Charity, Harvey Cedars, N.J. c. 1960. The Small estate eventually became the property of the Sisters of Charity of St. Elizabeth. Today it is known as Maris Stella and it serves as a place of summer retreat and vacations for the Sisters. $3-5

Cottages on Bay Front, Harvey Cedars, N.J. c. 1950. The cottage in the center, raised up on pilings, was the structure that started life as the High Point Yacht Club. $15-20

Public Dock, 74th Street, Harvey Cedars, N.J. July 11, 1939. Sent to Mrs. Ed Kunkle, Allentown, Pennsylvania. "My brother & I will come to see you as soon as I get home. The X shows me in a bathing suit. Mrs. Beitler." $20-25

Cottages Along Cedars Ave., Across Barnegat Bay, Harvey Cedars, N.J. c. 1950. $6-8

Picturesque Cove, Landmark of Harvey Cedars, New Jersey. c. 1965. $5-10

Barnegat Light Yacht Club and Anchorage, Harvey Cedars, New Jersey. c. 1950. $15-18

Ruins of the Ship's Wheel, Harvey Cedars. N.J. c. 1962. The Great March Storm of 1962 was even more devastating to Long Beach Island than the Hurricane of 1944 had been. Up and down the island, community after community was devastated by the storm. Nowhere were the destructive forces of this storm felt more than in the town of Harvey Cedars. At 79th Street, the forces of the storm cut through the deepest of a number of new inlets. Eventually this inlet would be closed, but not before it had completely cut off access to the north end of the island. $30-35

Destroyed home belonging to Paul L. Troast, Harvey Cedars, N.J. c. 1962. Caption on the reverse reads: "Destroyed home belonging to Paul L. Troast lies on the beach after successive high tides, which inundated this community, ripped out its foundations." Estimates were that up to half of the structures in Harvey Cedars had been lost to the storm. It would be years before the island would completely recover. $15-20

The U.S.S. Monssen Beached. c. 1962. On the reverse: "The Navy Destroyer USS Monssen lies aground where she was driven by gale winds and high tides March 6, 1962. Vessel remained aground until April 19, despite efforts of Navy salvage crews." The Monssen was being towed to Newport, Rhode Island, when in the midst of the storm, the cable snapped. She eventually went aground south of Beach Haven, one more victim of the Great Storm of 1962. $15-20

Between Harvey Cedars and Barnegat City is one more small enclave, and that is Loveladies. Today it too, like the Frazier Tract/North Beach, is a part of Long Beach Township. For years it was an undeveloped area that sported little more than a Life Saving Station. It was because of this Life Saving Station that the area derived its colorful name.

Thomas Lovelady was the owner of a small island in the bay known as Lovelady's Island. When the United States Life Saving Service wanted to name the station that it had established in this section of the island, there was no source to readily use as an identifier, as with Bond's Life Saving Station on the southern end of the island near the location of Captain Bond's Long Beach House. So they chose the next closest thing, Thomas Lovelady's Island, and named the station the Lovelady's Life Saving Station.

For decades this section of the island would informally be known as Lovelady's after the name of both the Life Saving Station and the island. When development began to change the wild sand dunes of Lovelady's into housing, and the bay was being dredged for lagoons, the name Long Beach Park began to be associated with the new developments around the Lovelady's Life Saving Station. Fortunately, this boring suburban name was soon dropped, the old name was modified, and forever after this enclave of large houses and open spaces has been known as Loveladies.

Loveladies Gift Shop, Harvey Cedars, N.J., Formerly Loveladies U.S. Coast Guard Station, Restored 1952. c. 1955. **The red houses were the earliest style of life saving station built at the New Jersey shore by the United States Life Saving Service. This former station located in Loveladies is a classic example of what is referred to as the New Jersey red-house-type station. After being in service for almost a century, the old building was restored and converted for use as a gift shop. $10-20**

The Long Beach Island Foundation for the Arts and Sciences, Loveladies, N.J. c. 1952. Founded in 1949 by artist Boris Blai, this non-profit organization provides arts and educational opportunities to island residents and visitors. $30-35

Loveladies Harbor, Harvey Cedars, N.J. c. 1959. Island land development had been going on for decades by the time this proposal came along. Located on the bay side of the island, the proposal called for the dredging of a main channel and radiating lagoons so that each homeowner could have their own private dock. With the opening of the Garden State Parkway, developments like this, and similar ones on the mainland, found a ready market of new homebuyers. $20-25

Chapter 12
Barnegat City and the Light That Never Fails

In 1878, an enterprising gentleman from Camden, New Jersey, arrived on the north end of Long Beach Island. Like the developers who came to the island before him, and like the many who have continued to come after, his head was filled with ideas when he recognized the potential that existed there amongst the cedars and sand dunes in the shadow of Barnegat lighthouse. His name was Benjamin F. Archer.

Although he was not the first to settle this area, he would be the most successful. Others had come before him, most notably Jacob Herring, who built a lodging establishment that he aptly named the Herring House. Because of its location, it primarily drew visitors from New York and northern New Jersey. But little else really developed in the area until Archer arrived on the scene. And by the time he did, the Herring House, by then renamed the Ashley House under new owners, was a relic of an earlier time, and when faced with the competition of Archer's planned hotels, it must have known its days were numbered.

In 1881, Archer laid out the town that he would name Barnegat City, and immediately set to work constructing the buildings that would make it a community. Under the aegis of his Barnegat City Beach Association he built first the Oceanic and then the Sans Souci Hotels.

The Oceanic was a monster of a place whose very distinctive roofline and double cupolas, constructed to hide water towers, were visible from both the mainland and from far out to sea. It was so large that it took two summers of building to complete. Constructed on the ocean side of Barnegat City, it was only meant to be used during the height of the summer season, as it would have been impossible to heat this gigantic place. So at the end of each season it was closed in anticipation of the next summer's round of activity.

The Sans Souci, built on the bay side of Barnegat City in 1883, was meant to be a year-round hotel. In the summer it would serve the people who were there for the beaches, and in the off season, it served the gunners who came for hunting. For Archer it was the best of both worlds.

In addition to the two hotels, Archer also began construction on a group of Victorian cottages, all of which were similar in design. They were tall, with peaked roofs and overhanging eaves. Adorned with gingerbread, they had beautiful porches across their fronts on both the first and second floors. A number of these cottages still exist, including the one that Benjamin Archer built for himself and his family.

The one thing that Archer did not really factor into his plans was the ever changing Barnegat Inlet. Like a shark, the inlet is constantly shifting and moving whether man wants it to or not, and it soon began to wreak havoc on Archer's Barnegat City. It probably didn't help that one of Archer's first moves in those environmentally unconscious days was to level Barnegat City's giant sand dunes, any beach community's first line of defense against the tides.

With each winter storm, the inlet shifted and the beach eroded further. One by one, Archer's Victorian cottages began to drop into the sea as whole streets were devoured by the encroaching waves. The Oceanic Hotel, which had twice been moved further inland from the approaching waves, finally dropped into the sea in the winter of 1920.

By the time that the Oceanic fell, it had not been open for a great number of years. Archer's Barnegat City had never quite taken off the way many of the other beach communities on the island did, and as a result, the Oceanic Hotel had basically just been abandoned. Rail service to the north end of LBI was sporadic at best, and that undoubtedly contributed to its decline. It seems that most visitors to the island wanted to head south to Beach Haven where all the action was taking place, rather than to ramshackle Barnegat City.

Today, a great portion of Archer's original settlement of Barnegat City has disappeared completely with the vagaries of the shifting inlet. Barnegat Light was adopted as the town's name in 1948, officially ending Benjamin Archer's dreams of grandeur for his Barnegat City.

Birds Eye View of Barnegat City, N.J. from Top of Lighthouse. c. 1910. This view looks east from the top of Barnegat Lighthouse over Benjamin Archer's Barnegat City. Just to the left of center is the Oceanic Hotel with its twin cupolas. It had already been moved back twice from the original location by the time this photo was taken. Much of what you see here has since been swallowed by the sea. Sent to Mr. Lewis Smith, St. Joseph, Mo. March 22, 1910. "This is not the cottage but a duplicate of the one I offer. The owner occupies this one." On back, from 330, N. 6th St, Camden N.J.: "I am sorry this picture with cottage marked is the best I have now. The beach for beauty as well as safety cannot be surpassed. A family is absolutely safe here in every way. We are too primitive for plumbing & no cottage is thus equipped. There is a good cistern, which supplies ample & satisfactory water from which no trouble has ever arisen. Will be glad to further answer questions. (Mrs.) E.K. Archer." $50-100

The Sunset Inn from Top of Lighthouse, Barnegat City, N.J. c. 1910. This is the companion view to the previous image, looking west over the sedge islands to the mainland. In the Foreground is the Sunset Hotel, formerly the Sans Souci, Benjamin Archer's year-round hostelry. $50-100

Sunset Inn from the Bay, Barnegat City, N.J. c. 1908. Archer sold the Sans Souci in 1887. The new owners changed the name to the Sunset Inn. In this real photo postcard, notice the house that sits in front of the hotel, on the bay. The style of this home is typical of those that Archer built in Barnegat City. The windmill behind the house would have been used to pump water from an artesian well. $100

SUNSET HOTEL, BARNEGAT CITY, N. J.

Sunset Hotel, Barnegat City, N.J. c. 1930. Successive owners modernized and updated the old Sunset Hotel in hopes that business would return to Barnegat City. All that came to end on the night of June 26, 1932, when the old hotel burned to the ground in a fire that could be seen for miles. $80-90

Little Fishermen from Sunset Inn, Barnegat City, N. J.

SUNSET WHARF, BARNEGAT CITY, N. J.

Sunset Wharf, Barnegat City, N.J. c. 1925. $40

Little Fishermen from Sunset Inn, Barnegat City, N.J. c. 1907. Because it was open all year, the Sunset was a favorite of the gunning and fishing crowd. Here two of her youngest patrons show off their prize catch. $200

The Social, Barnegat City, N.J. c. 1907. This real photo postcard shows The Social, a popular boardinghouse that was run by the Kroger family. Many small establishments such as this existed in the beach towns of Long Beach Island. $40-60

Fourth Street, Barnegat City, N.J. c. 1925. The building on the left did double duty as Barnegat City's general store and post office. $60-80

Photograph. c. 1907. People come to the shore to have fun. That is something that doesn't change. These folks seem to be having a high old time pulling their express wagon through the streets of Barnegat City. $40-50

Barnegat City Tea Shop
Central Ave. and 8th St.   Barnegat City, N. J.

Barnegat City Tea Shop, Central Ave. and 8th St., Barnegat City, N.J. c. 1920. On reverse: "You will be glad to know that the Barnegat City Tea Shop has been enlarged and the Dining Room and Service improved in every way; the sleeping quarters are also much improved. Our shower baths are first class. Opens for the Season on May 28. Mrs. Magna Hansen, Tel. Beach Haven 31-R-31. Fishing Parties accommodated." $40-60

Zion Lutheran Church of Long Beach Island, 18th and Central Avenues, Barnegat Light, N.J. c. 1965. $3-5

Barnegat L.S.S. No. 17. c. 1905. Sent to Samuel Morton, Avalon, N.J. L.S.S. This extremely rare real photo postcard shows the Barnegat City Life Saving Station of the U.S. Life Saving Service. It is what is referred to as an 1882-type station that was greatly expanded. Another card from the same sender identifies him as A.E. Bunnell, most likely a member of the Barnegat Life Saving Station crew, and he tells the recipient to "Remember me to Capt and Mrs. Swain." $200

Barnegat Light Motel, Broadway & 7th St., Barnegat Light, N.J. c. 1960. By the 1950s, motels were springing up in many of Long Beach Island's communities. Barnegat Light was no exception. This place advertised that they were open from April 1 to November 15 and the sender noted on the back that the cost was $14 per day. $5-8

Sea Splash Motel, Barnegat Light, Long Beach Island, N.J. c. 1965. $5-8

Barnegat Light, N.J. c. 1955. This mid-century view of Barnegat Lighthouse, and of the community that was renamed in her honor, shows the extent to which the inlet has eaten away at the northern end of the island. Compare this with the first view in this chapter and you will understand the enormous power of the ocean to wreak destruction on man's creations. $5-8

The Crash of the U.S.S. Akron (La caduta nell'oceano in tempesta dell' "Akron", il piu grande dirigibile Americano). From *La Domenica del Corriere,* an Italian newsmagazine, April 16, 1933. Barnegat City's greatest brush with fame came on the night of April 4, 1933, when the U.S. Navy's lighter-than-air ship, known as the *Akron,* crashed into the storm-tossed sea eighteen miles off her shore. On board at the time were a number of important naval commanders including Rear Admiral William Moffett, a man considered to be the father of naval aviation. All but three of her crew perished in the crash. The ensuing search and rescue operations focused much attention on Barnegat City and on Long Beach Island. $10-20

The Light That Never Fails

Long before there was a Barnegat City, there was a Barnegat Light. With a long history of disastrous shipwrecks off its shores, the United States Government decided to build a light on LBI. The original Barnegat Lighthouse was built in 1834. While it served a purpose, it was only marginally effective since it had a steady light rather than a rotating one, and it often misled mariners into believing that it was another ship on the horizon. Its history would be short-lived. Again, the shifting tides and the ever-moving inlet began their nefarious work. By 1850, the base of the lighthouse had been gnawed away, and the foundations were in danger of being undermined.

The branch of the government that oversees the construction and operation of the country's lighthouses recognized that it needed to do something before the light was lost. Acknowledging that the old light was not the most effective, it came up with a design for a new lighthouse that would far surpass the old one in both size and in the light it could produce. Construction was begun in 1856 under the supervision of George Gordon Meade, who would later go on to Civil War fame at the Battle of Gettysburg.

The lighthouse that was constructed outshone its predecessor in design and operation. It cast a light that could be seen as far as twenty miles out to sea. It was commissioned in January of 1859, which was a good thing since the old lighthouse had tumbled into the sea part way through construction of the new one, and it continued to serve the needs of ships at sea until it was decommissioned and replaced by the Barnegat Lightship in 1927.

Barnegat Lighthouse, affectionately referred to as Old Barney, has become an icon. She is the one symbol that is most closely identified with Long Beach Island. Her familiar red and white pattern of paint is immediately recognizable to anyone who has ever seen it. Her iconographic image has appeared on everything from bank checks to calendars to milk bottles, and continues to appear on thousands of other souvenirs year after year. Since the earliest days of the postcard, publishers have been capturing and producing her image. Here follows just a small selection of the hundreds of postcards that have appeared during the last century.

Barnegat Light House. c. 1908. **Visible to the right of the lighthouse is the huge lighthouse keeper's house that the Federal Lighthouse Bureau built in 1889. Built to look like one large structure, it was actually three separate homes that were all connected to one another. $20**

Barnegat Lighthouse, Barnegat City, N.J. c. 1905. **This is an even better view of the lighthouse keeper's house for understanding just how big this building was. Sadly, this structure would not last long enough to see its 35th birthday. $70-90**

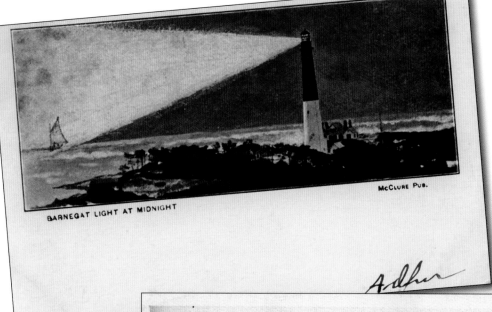

BARNEGAT LIGHT AT MIDNIGHT

McClure Pub.

Barnegat Light at Midnight, McClure Pub. c. 1906. Barnegat's beam could be seen twenty miles out to sea. This dramatic rendering shows her lighting the way for a ship sailing past LBI. $20

Barnegat Light, Barnegat City, N.J., April 15th, 1920. c. 1920. In April of 1920, the same storm that had brought down the Oceanic Hotel chewed away at the foundations of the lighthouse keeper's house. Rather than try to save it, the Lighthouse Bureau put it up for auction with the proviso that the owner had to demolish it. The structure was sold for $160 and was subsequently removed. $70-90

Barnegat Light, Barnegat City, N. J., April 15th, 1920

Barnegat Light, New Jersey

Barnegat Light, New Jersey. c. 1930. $15-25

Real Photo Postcard: Barnegat Light House. c. 1920. This real photo postcard image of the Barnegat Lighthouse is by a photographer who only signed his work with an interlocking RP. He seems to have taken a number of photos in Barnegat City around the mid-1920s. $50-70

Visit Spray Beach, Six-Miles at Sea, Barnegat Light, Barnegat City, N.J. c. 1935. Although Barnegat Lighthouse is in Barnegat Light, that has not stopped every other community on Long Beach Island from co-opting it as their own for publicity purposes. Postcard publishers have done the same. Many examples of this exist, like this card, pictured here. $10-15

Advertising Calendar, Whalon's on Long Beach Island for the year 1949. $10-15

The Light House Barnegat City, N.J. c. 1940. $10-15

The Fabulous Barnegat Light. c. 1944. $10-15

Aerial View of Barnegat Light, N.J. c. 1950. After the storms of 1920, and the loss of the lighthouse keeper's house, it was feared that Old Barney would be the next to fall into the ocean. The government, ready to commission a new lightship, could have cared less. This time, though, the citizens of Barnegat City, and all those that loved the lighthouse, rose up in righteous indignation over the fact that nothing was being done to preserve her. Eventually jetties were built to stop the erosion at the base of the light. $4-8

Barnegat Light, N.J. c. 1950. $4-8

Barnegat Light, Ship Bottom-Beach Arlington, N.J.
c. 1941. $10-15

Barnegat Lighthouse, Built 1858, Now New Jersey State Park. c. **1967.** **$4-8**

Barnegat Light at Night, Barnegat Light, N.J. c. **1950. On the reverse: "The poet Deets says, 'As a beacon of mercy Old Barnegat stood at the edge of the bay; beyond the pinewood. Sending its beacon far over the sea; to guide the poor fisherman or you or me'." $4-8**

Barnegat Light Inlet, Barnegat Light, N.J. c. 1950. Just like their ancestors at the Sunset Wharf, people are still fishing from the piers at Barnegat Light. $2-5

Barnegat Light House. c. 1969. On the reverse: "The New Jersey and Long Beach Island flags are prominently flown over the pathway leading to historic Barnegat Light." $2-5

Fishing Off The Pier at Barnegat Light, N.J. c. 1960. $2-5

Bibliography

Brinckmann, John. *The Tuckerton Railroad*. New Jersey, 1973.

Brown, John K. *The Baldwin Locomotive Works, 1831-1915: A Study in American Industrial Practice*. Baltimore, Maryland: The Johns Hopkins University Press, 1995.

Bucholz, Margaret Thomas. *Seasons in the Sun: A Photographic History of Harvey Cedars: 1894-1947*. New Jersey, 1994.

Handschuch, Richard, and Sal Marino. *The Beach Bum's Guide to the Boardwalks of New Jersey*. Beach Haven, New Jersey: Beach Bum Press, 2000.

Hartnett, George C. and Kevin Hughes. *Long Beach Island*. Portsmouth, New Hampshire: Arcadia Publishing, 2004.

Hughes, Kevin. *Barnegat: Life By The Bay*. Dover, New Hampshire: Arcadia Publishing, 1997.

Kane, B.; M. Meredith; and E. Kane. *50th Anniversary of Beach Haven Terrace: 1907-1957*. New Jersey, 1957.

Lloyd, John Bailey. *Eighteen Miles of History on Long Beach Island*. Harvey Cedars, New Jersey: Down The Shore Publishing, 1994.

Lloyd, John Bailey. *Six Miles at Sea: A Pictorial History of Long Beach Island, N.J.* Harvey Cedars, New Jersey: Down The Shore Publishing, 1990.

Nash, Charles Edgar. *The Lure of Long Beach*. Long Beach Island, New Jersey: The Long Beach Board of Trade, 1936.

Ocean County Sun, "The Great March Storm, 1962."

Phillips, Steven J. *Old House Dictionary*. Washington, D.C.: The Preservation Press, 1994.

Savadove, Larry, and Margaret Thomas Bucholz. *Great Storms of the Jersey Shore*. Harvey Cedars, New Jersey: Down The Shore Publishing, 1993.

Shanks, Ralph, Wick York, and Lisa Woo Shanks, editor. *U.S. Life-Saving Service: Heroes, Rescues & Architecture of the Early Coast Guard*. Petaluma, California: Costano Books, 1996.

Somerville, George B. *The Lure of Long Beach*. Long Beach, New Jersey: Long Beach Board of Trade, 1914.